Mango Days

DATE DUE

Patty at age 17 nears the 25-mile mark in the Honolulu Marathon.

(Cover photo was taken six months later at her senior prom—several weeks after she had started chemotherapy.)

Mango Days

A Teenager Facing Eternity
Reflects on the Beauty of Life

PATTY SMITH

Hope Publishing House
Pasadena, California

Copyright © 1993 by Marjorie N. Smith & Christopher C. Smith

Hope Publishing House
P. O. Box 60008
Pasadena, California 91116 - U.S.A.
Telephone (818) 792-6123; FAX (818) 792-2121

Cover design - Christina Rodriguez

Printed in the U.S.A. on acid-free paper.

Second printing 1994, revised

Library of Congress Cataloging-in-Publication Data

Smith, Patty, 1962-1981.
     Mango days : a teenager facing eternity reflects on the beauty
of life / writings of Patty Smith.
          p.   cm.
     ISBN 0-932727-59-X (lib. bdg.) : $17.95 — ISBN 0-932727-58-1
(paper) : $11.95
        1. Smith, Patty, 1962-1981—Health. 2. Tumors in adolescence—
Patients—United States—Diaries. I. Title.
RC265.6.S65A3 1992
362.1'9699442'0092—dc20
[B]   92-10039
                                             CIP

"Sometime before I leave I will write my 'Mango Days.' These are my mango days, Susie. I'm not sure exactly how the metaphor will work, but my summer seems bound to that exquisite, sweet, opulent orange fruit. . . ."

[from a letter to friend Susie Chun written July 23, 1980–four months after Patty learned she had cancer, two months before she left for college and eleven months before she died. The poem never was written.]

Acknowledgments

Margie and I, Patty's parents, owe thanks to many people for helping to bring this book from idea to reality:

To Susie Chun, Patty's kindred spirit and special friend, who remarkably kept all the letters Patty wrote to her and who loaned them to us to make copies.

To Alan Shapiro, who as an English teacher at Stanford University found in Patty a student who read poems as "matters of life and death" rather than as mere assignments and "who paid meticulous attention to what she read, more than any student I have ever known." Those words, contained in a 1984 essay he wrote for Northwestern University's literary publication, encouraged us to share Patty's story.

To Betty Skinsnes, who happened to see one of Patty's poems—"hauntingly beautiful" she called it—and has used it in teaching in China about death and dying in America. (The poem appears in Chapter 15.) Betty put us in touch with Children's Hospice International of Alexandria, Va., an organization dedicated to support and care for children with life-threatening conditions.

To the staff at Children's Hospice International and particularly Patricia Dailey and Wendy Bailey, who worked hard to find a publisher.

To Faith Annette Sand, publisher of Hope Publishing House, who perceived in the manuscript "almost an Anne Frank quality" (a reference to the moving diary written five decades ago) and agreed with enthusiasm to take on the project.

To Paul "Doc" Berry and William Messer, Patty's two favorite teachers at Punahou School, who read the manuscript with care and made helpful suggestions regarding the introductory pages.

To Patty's sisters, Suzanne and Sandy, who besides useful ideas have given unfailing love and support.

—Christopher (Kit) and Margie Smith
594-B Hahaione St.
Honolulu, HI 96825

Note: *Patty's writings selected for this book stand unedited, as 100 percent hers. The sketches used throughout the book also are hers.*

And whence is courage. . . . that
in misfortune, even death,
encourages others
and in its defeat, stirs

the soul to be strong.

—Marianne Moore

(from the poem, "What are Years?")

Preface

This entry may shock you. I have to talk about this, though.

I have cancer. No kidding, I just found out today. I'm really having a hard time believing it, but somehow I think I expected it all along.

I don't know how bad it is. I keep telling myself they may have made a mistake. Stage 1 — Denial.

The date was March 28, 1980; time—late evening. Patty, then 17, was writing in her journal for a Humanities course at Punahou School in Honolulu.

Earlier, Margie and I had hosted dinner guests from the Mainland. Patty and her 15-year-old sister Sandy had gone out separately with friends. Sister Suzy, 19, was in California at college. Outwardly, this would have seemed an ordinary Friday evening of an essentially happy, well-adjusted, middle-class family.

Just that day, however, we had learned that Patty had malignant non-Hodgkin's lymphoma. The doctor had called with a biopsy report on a tumor removed from her left forearm. Margie had agreed to tell Patty on a walk after the guests had left. I hadn't the courage to go along.

The report of course had devastated us. God had given us three wonderful daughters, each a special joy in her own way. For us, too, Stage 1 was denial.

Over the next 15 months, we were to experience in waves numerous emotions: Fear. Hope. Helplessness.

Questioning. (Had we not fed her properly? Were the doctors doing all the right things? And, to God, *Why?*). And, in big portions, gratitude, for outpourings of love and support. We felt pain, too, of course, although one becomes aware that pain as the cancer victim suffers it can barely be understood by others. Then there's simple fatigue; as her pain intensified, our endurance as care-givers sometimes faltered.

As for the spiritual dimension, such experiences become double-or-nothing affairs. Either your faith in God dries up in a sense of abandonment or it deepens in confidence that this life, precious though it may be, comprises just a chapter in our loving Creator's eternal plan. Amidst all our questioning, our faith as Christians grew.

Patty's remarkable attitude of acceptance supported us. As she told a much-admired former teacher a few weeks before she died, she saw her story as about how people find the courage to do what life requires of them and how, given one chance, you have to do it as well as you can. Everyone is entitled, she added, to some less-than-noble moments along the way.

Back to her journal:

> I called Debbie as soon as I found out. We had just gotten back from the symphony. . . .
> I'm glad I called Deb. She didn't burst into tears but calmed me down. She said to call her anytime, anywhere. I really don't like the idea of telling my friends, but I have to. I would feel terrible if one of my friends had cancer and didn't tell me.
> I'm so glad I'm not an atheist. My mother, in a fit of superstition for which I scolded her, flipped open the Bible immediately when she heard the news from the doctor. She found a neat verse

though:

"The Lord told Moses not to fear—that the enemy was already conquered."

I certainly hope that's appropriate.

Anyway I don't know what to do about telling people. I don't want to hide it, but then again I don't want everyone to feel so sorry for me that they don't act natural. I don't want any "let's be nice to Pat in case she dies" business. But it probably can't be avoided.

I'm surprised I'm taking this so well. I have to make sure I stay strong. I have to make sure my family doesn't fall apart. I want to keep calm and not get too dramatic about this. I'm sure God knows what God is doing. I will accept this situation. I will choose it. I will probably cry and scream and I may be a bit bitter for a while. But I will conquer this. I will be strong no matter what I find out on Monday. Strong with the help of God.

On Monday we took Patty to see Dr. John Mueh (pronounced "Mee"), the oncologist at Kaiser Foundation Hospital in Honolulu. She immediately liked and respected him, the beginning of a reserved mutual admiration that was to grow in the months ahead.

"I'm very concerned about you," Dr. Mueh told her that day. But he gave us news that, for the moment, flooded us with relief. Non-Hodgkin's lymphoma is a curable form of cancer, he said—thanks to chemotherapy.

In consultation with doctors at Stanford University, Dr. Mueh prescribed a chemotherapy called "CHOP" (shorthand for the four drugs used). Within weeks, however, it became clear her body wasn't responding.

Nevertheless, she went off to California, despite periods of severe pain, to enroll at Stanford University as a freshman. Her first stop was at Stanford Medical Center, which has one of the world's top lymphoma clinics. The doctors minced no words; yes, they said, she might die.

An aggressive new chemotherapy kept a lid on the disease for a time and again we allowed ourselves hope. In fact, when Patty flew home for Christmas she seemed well, despite an expected total loss of hair due to chemotherapy. Several weeks later her critical blood counts were the best in months.

But then in March (1981) came what Patty called a "good news, bad news" phone call—the good news an A on a paper, the bad news that lymphoma spots seemed to be coming back. Several days later, we got a call from one of her doctors. Patty's condition had "plummeted," the doctor said, and given the best of all worlds, she only had months.

Still, they made one last try at yet another chemotherapy, keeping Patty in Stanford Hospital five weeks. Finally Patty said "enough," and she came home to Hawaii in May. She died June 20 in Kaiser Hospital after several days there.

Those last days included visits with the friends about whom she had written often in her journal. These were good-byes, and all knew it.

Patty's closest friend during most of her illness was Susie Chun, with whom she had worked on the Punahou School yearbook, *The Oahuan.* Susie was the over-all editor, Patty the copy editor. During the last year of Patty's life, the two corresponded frequently, even while both were home during the summer of 1980, preparing to go off to college.

That fall, eight months before she died, Patty wrote to Susie from Stanford after hearing welcoming speeches to the recently arrived freshmen. She had undergone a bone marrow biopsy that day and admitted to worry: "I know I shouldn't worry," she said. "But how can I not worry?"

Later in the letter she said:

The speeches actually inspired me. I still want to work toward a career in journalism, but now I don't think so much about the future. I will instead pursue intellectual kicks, the high of reading a poem and actually understanding it, the quiet ecstasy of a paper written well. I don't want to seem morbid, but I must accept the very real possibility of death. And keep my faith.

Whether I die next year or live to a hundred, I want to create something lasting before I go. I suppose that's why people have children. I don't know what exactly I mean by "lasting." I just have this vague (and very human) urge.

It's that last paragraph, I think, that led us to put together this book. In reading her journals, her poems and her letters to Susie, we came to believe that Patty had a lot to say to others besides teachers and a best friend—particularly to people facing life-threatening diseases. From a perspective a healthy person can barely imagine, Patty tells of life's joys, it heartaches, its puzzlements, its ultimate meaning.

When in God's mercy and goodness Patty and I are reunited in God's heavenly realm, I may well get a scolding from her. On the front page of one journal—one she kept for herself rather than for a class—she wrote: "NOTE: Anyone would scorn to read this without permission if he/she had the decency and/or soul of a flea. . . . Hopefully, this means you." On the other hand, in a July 1, 1980, letter to Susie she wrote: "Writing without a reader is like acting without an audience—dull and rather purposeless."

I have tried to omit that which might be truly personal. If I have failed in that, forgive me, Patty.

May this be your "Mango Days," a part of the "something lasting" you had in mind.

—Kit Smith

Prologue

Nowadays couples seem to delay both getting married and starting families. By contrast, Margie and I married when she was 20 and I was 24. Before she reached 26, we had three daughters.

We had the same concerns as all parents that our children would be born healthy. But we both had experienced happy relationships with loving families and neither of us had lost a parent or sibling. So we looked forward to child rearing with confidence and a sense of joy-filled adventure.

Patty—Patricia Louise—was born August 31, 1962, in San Diego, California. As with Suzy, the first-born, and Sandy later, we talked and shared with her right from the start, including songs and word games and reading. Margie, then a full-time homemaker (she is now a librarian), began reading to Patty virtually as soon as she could prop her up in her lap.

While each daughter responded enthusiastically, in Patty's case words were to become the central element in her life—first in reading, then in writing and later in good conversation. As a teenager she wrote in her journal: "I wonder if I was born loving words," and "To me words mean power."

At age two, Patty could identify the numerous kinds of dinosaurs and upon request would do so with great delight—"tyrannosaurus," "stegosaurus," "triceratops"— the whole list. Watching the "Sesame Street" TV show, she would memorize rhyming songs consisting of numerous verses.

And she was creative, even before she could write. At nursery school, she so enjoyed mixing colors that one day when Margie arrived to pick her up, Patty was still happily at work finger-painting, her arms covered up to her elbows with the combination of colors. When a sock would disappear from my drawer, it would turn up fashioned into a turtleneck sweater for a teddy bear or something equally imaginative. Later she would take that sock's mate, this time with a clear conscience; what use was there, she explained, for an odd sock?

After living three years in Los Angeles, we moved in 1971 to Honolulu, Hawaii, my birthplace. I had obtained a job at the morning newspaper, *The Honolulu Advertiser,* covering business news, a job I still hold.

By now Patty read voraciously. She would read anywhere and anytime she could. Once, riding the bus home from school, she became so absorbed in a book that she failed to get off at the right stop. Getting off finally in an unfamiliar neighborhood, she must have looked very lost; a kind lady spotted her and gave her a ride home.

Patty's reading stirred in her an interest in Britain's Royal Family and I drew on that to work out a bribe. I love sports and wanted Patty and Sandy to go out for Bobby Sox softball. Patty balked; athletics didn't come easily to her. What could I offer as an inducement? She suggested a subscription to the *Illustrated London News*— by air mail. She had a deal.

Dutifully Patty put in her year as a Bobby Soxer, warming the bench except for playing the minimum two innings per game that Bobby Sox rules require. But she came to care a lot for her teammates and she rooted hard for them.

Before her teen years, she would read and reread ten to 15 good-sized books every two weeks. I hadn't realized how quickly she read until once on a flight from Honolulu to California I watched her devour an entire novel, Arthur Hailey's *Runway Zero-Eight*.

"In a way the books became my society," she would later write in a journal. "I got a lot of my values from imaginary peers." Her favorite was *The Lord of the Rings*, a trilogy by British author J.R.R. Tolkien, which she read eleven times.

Patty felt that being the middle child held mixed blessings. Older sister Suzy "resented me from birth, for about 13 years," she later wrote. Suzy would push for attention, and usually get it, Patty thought—and she had a point. But the situation had a plus side, Patty said: "It made me more tolerant, calm and easy-going. It also made me a little insecure, but I'd rather be insecure than overconfident."

For her part, Suzy may have been sensitive about her size. At an early age, Patty passed her older sister in height, as did Sandy. Suzy stopped growing at five feet. Often Patty was taken as oldest of the three.

Patty also felt her childhood was shaped by what she would call "the ugliness factor." "Relatives used to comment on Sandy's cuteness, Suzy's prettiness. Then they'd look at me and tell me how smart I was. It just wasn't the same. So I grew up valuing intelligence over looks—who wants to value what they don't have over what they do (supposedly)?"

Typically, Patty's teenage years were a period of exploration—not only of reading and writing but of music, running and, yes, of boys. As a ninth-grader she had a steady boyfriend—a senior tuba player! Her grades were poor that year, but no doubt she gained perspective and maturity.

Patty played the trombone, which she had taken up in junior high. I had begun playing the trombone three decades earlier at the same school (and still play), so it warmed my heart that she chose it. Few girls do.

Because softball had been less than a thrilling

experience for Patty, it surprised us when she developed an interest in running. "Running takes a lot of time, but it also helps me organize my thoughts," she wrote later on a college application, telling of her nonacademic interests. It also provided a release from frustrations after a trying day, she said, and helped her to get to know others. "I've had many of my best conversations on the run."

Furthermore, Patty had become terribly weight-conscious—needlessly, really—and saw running as a way of burning calories. She became a semi-vegetarian, with tofu as her staple source of protein. We feared at one point she had tilted toward anorexia nervosa as she dropped to about 105 pounds—much too light for her five-foot, seven-inch frame.

Patty had no idea of doing terribly well as a runner. She had a severely pronated (flat) right foot, which caused some pain, evidenced by a tendency to wear out running shoes quickly. Nevertheless she set as a goal the running of a marathon, 26.2 miles long, and in December 1979 she achieved that at the seventh annual Honolulu Marathon. It was a family affair; sister Sandy and I ran, too.

Writing for the school newspaper, *Ka Punahou,* she wrote about her marathon experience, its agonies and its joys:

> At the 13-mile mark, pain had begun to settle in my limbs and one foot throbbed mercilessly.
>
> At the next aid station, I took off my shoe for a quick glance. The toe of my sock was red with blood. I shoved my shoe back on and tried to pretend I hadn't seen anything. . . . I hit the finish line at four hours and 34 minutes. As a cheerful Jaycee hosed me off, I shivered with joy and relief. Even now, I can't believe I finished. At least, not until I try to move my legs.

Later we would realize that Patty had run the 26.2 miles with at least two tumors—the one on her left forearm and another on her right buttock.

As a senior, she went out for the track team, and her attitude of acceptance was put to the test as she suffered pains in her ankles, shins and knees. Because recovery seemed improbable, the coach asked her to become a manager. "After feeling angry and upset about my inability to compete, I grew to enjoy the satisfaction of managing the team and purged myself of any bitterness," she wrote in an English class paper. "I 'chose' to manage the team and thus turned my injury into a positive experience."

Patty's interest in writing had begun with poetry, long before her running. She had submitted several poems to the British children's publication, *Puffin Post*, and three were published. In high school she worked on *The Oahuan*, the school yearbook, as well as *Ka Punahou*.

What event most influenced her life? Asked that question on a college application, Patty wrote about her participation the previous summer in an expedition for Earthwatch, a nonprofit sponsor of archaeological, scientific and environmental projects using mainly volunteers. Patty had chosen an archaeological "dig" in Strichen, Scotland, the site of an ancient stone circle, a mini-version of the famed Stonehenge in southern England.

"While I learned a lot from the dig itself, I learned even more from my journey to the site and the people I met along the way," she said.

I arrived in London's Heathrow Airport feeling friendless and confused. But when I wandered through customs to the main lobby, cousins I'd never seen greeted me with signs bearing my name. They insisted I stay with them and they took me through London, Oxford and Windsor.

Their neighbors invited me to teas, picnics and dinner and saw me off at the train station when I left for Scotland.

(Ironically, one of the cousins, her grandfather's first cousin, later was diagnosed as having non-Hodgkin's lymphoma, the same disease Patty had. In his case, chemotherapy would be successful.)

Total strangers showed the same warm concern, from the Canadian youth hostelers who helped me when I missed my train in Edinburgh to the Scottish girl whose parents drove me to my Aberdeen hotel. The kind treatment I met everywhere increased my faith in human nature and the world at large.

I also gained faith in my own abilities. The crises I faced in a foreign country made me realize that I could cope on my own. . . .

Her Earthwatch experience inspired this exercise, typical of Patty, in whimsy and irony:

Strichen

I get another sweater on
I add an extra shirt
I ride out to the windy hill
And grovel in the dirt

The rain beats fiercely on my back
My lips turn slowly blue
I ponder the significance
Of troweling worms in two

Then just as I get interested
And trowel away with glee
I have to clear up all my loose
And stagger down to tea

I wake up from my teatime nap
But the break still isn't through
I put away my plastic cup
And join the dovecot queue

The clock creeps round till five o'clock
When ends the weary day
I clear up all my loose again
And put my tools away

I climb into the crowded van
A weary muddy slob
I wonder for the millionth time
What made me choose this job.

Patty's most tangible success as a writer came in her
senior year at Punahou. Being a pushy father, I had
urged her as a junior to enter an economics essay contest
sponsored by Castle & Cooke Inc. (now known as Dole
Food Co.), one of Hawaii's largest corporations. She had
begged off, promising she would as a senior. O.K., I
agreed. And this time no need for a bribe!

I was sensitive, naturally, to any notion I might have
helped her. The fact is I didn't see the essay until it was
published as the winning entry in the *Honolulu Star-
Bulletin*, which, ironically, competes with my newspaper,
The Advertiser. Patty's prize was $2,500—quite a morale
booster for someone who had learned of her cancer only
weeks before.

The assigned topic was "Profit—Is it Really a Four-

Letter Word?" Her conclusion: "Without profits to finance development, the economy would stagnate. And people need the incentive of profit to make them do their best."

She had finished the essay at the *Oahuan* office at school. "If I win," she told her fellow staffers in a burst of relief, "I'll take all you guys out to dinner." I gulped but she honored that pledge without hesitation. She picked up the tab for the 25 or so who joined her at Dickens Pub for virgin daiquiris and dinner.

That summer, as a diversion, Patty joined Susie Chun in staging "Hawaii's First Boggle Tournament." As wordsmiths, Susie and Pat had become great fans of Boggle, a mind-stretching word game from Parker Brothers.

The two youthful promoters went all out. They got city permission to use Thomas Square, a public park near downtown; they fixed the registration at 32 and prepared posters and press releases; and they purchased tasteful wooden bowls for the winners as well as "Boggle 1980" pins and refreshments for all the entrants. Needless to say, the $2.50 entry fee didn't cover costs, but the tournament plainly was an artistic success.

I recall well that Patty was a sick girl that day, hurting as the lymphoma had worked into her bones. She had to lie down several times on the grass and after the tournament I took her to see Dr. Mueh.

The next year her friends, obviously very special people, would stage another Boggle tournament at the very same corner of Thomas Square. Across the top of the entry form was printed: "In Memoriam—Patricia Smith."

1

From this point, Patty's own words tell her story of coping with cancer. While her writing provides a chronology, I have added occasional notes by way of explanation.

The first three chapters consist of entries in the journal she kept as a Humanities course project for school. The first entry comes just a month before her visit to the doctor to see about an "ugly greenish bump" on her forearm. Knowledge of her cancer is two months away, but even here Patty plainly grasps the preciousness of life and its finiteness.

Patty's letters to Susie Chun begin in Chapter 5.

Her poems are interspersed throughout, not necessarily at the points in time they were written. The poems, unfortunately, were not dated.

Some of the journal entries refer to a book read by the class, The Mountain People by Colin M. Turnbull, about the Ik (pronounced "Eek"), a tribe of African herdsmen. The Ik's history took a dark turn as they began to delight in misfortunes of others. Turnbull says they lost their capacity for goodness, truth and beauty, willingly abandoning these "virtues" as useless baggage. Eventually the entire tribe perished.

January 1980 —

The idea of keeping a journal both excites and frightens me. I love to write and enjoy expressing my thoughts in journal entries and poems, but usually nobody else sees what I write unless they're a very close friend. Writing casually for a grade worries me— will I say the "wrong" thing? Will I bore you? Will you think I'm odd, or dull, or worst of all, ordinary?

I have no choice—I have to write this—so I can only hope my self-consciousness will vanish with time.

My older sister told me I would hate *The Mountain People,* because I'm too optimistic. I don't hate it yet . . . maybe I'm not as optimistic as she thought.

I have to agree with Turnbull's assertion that human "virtues" are luxuries, affordable only in a secure, well-fed society. Yet I rebel when he says that they hinder survival, probably because I define survival as more than a beating heart and a functioning brain. Survival, to me, means the retention of human dignity—keeping a moral code or at least a rough outline of one, being able to love others.

I know that my definition of survival isn't "correct" in dictionary terms or even where most other people are concerned. I'm thinking of the survival of *humans.* Living, eating, breathing, the Ik are certainly surviving (if precariously) as animals. Yet as humans they are dying out. I think that the loving Kauar, though he died in his prime, lived, as a human, longer than any other Ik.

January 23, 1980 —

Today I had my first seminar. The hypothetical situation about the nuclear radiation and the limited food really made me think about my own values.

I said that I would walk out, in a sense kill myself,

to leave more food for the others. Naturally, I was in the minority. Yet I really meant what I said; I know that for me, the sacrifice would be instinctive, my first impulse. I explained that for me, the quality of life means far more than its duration. Living in a room of vicious, starving people would be hellish and I'd rather die in an attempt to prevent that hell than I would live in it. . . .

I suppose that the situation we discussed is much like that of the Ik. The nine survivors would be the most egocentric and callous, the most willing to snatch food from others or push weaker people out the door. They would have to steel themselves against the weakening emotions of love and compassion, and value the food above all else.

That's what happened to the Ik. Loving people like Kauar and Abdula die. The conniving and uncaring profit from their death and remain alive. Food becomes a religion to them—their only true value or concern.

I don't mean to insult the people who said they would stay and fight for the food and I don't think I'm any better a person for deciding to leave. If we didn't have people who believed in survival despite all costs, we wouldn't have a race now—crises would have wiped us out a long time ago.

January 26, 1980 —
We talked about identity in seminar the other day and I happily wrote "I am happy with myself and my world." You said that we'd change our minds in three weeks. I changed mine in a day. I now feel extremely depressed, like someone kicked me on the tip of the chin.

Yet I'm not sure why. I know what triggered my depression. I was laughing about a headline for an

Oahuan spread and saying very silly things. Suddenly Susie snapped at me and said I was being very silly. I was, and she was right, and I don't know if she was really mad at me or just felt grumpy. Anyway, I suddenly felt like crying. And now, I still feel that way. But why? That's a very minor incident. I must have a very shaky identity if something that small can bother me this much. And *that* makes me feel worse.

I've noticed that I depend a lot on other people for my self-esteem. I'm like a puppy that needs to be told it's a good dog every three minutes, I guess. Anyway, when someone compliments me or shows concern about something, I think I'm a very independent person who doesn't really need the reassurance. It's only when I've been insulted or ignored that I realize how insecure I am. Maybe this will help me remember how much I need other people.

January 27, 1980 —
Now that I read what I wrote yesterday, I want to rip out the page. I always want to rip out depressing pages. I guess we do the same thing in our minds— eliminate the sad incidents and only remember the fun parts or the interesting parts. Now, as I think about last night (actually yesterday morning), I only remember isolated incidents. It seems like a bad dream. We worked [on *Oahuan*] until 5:30 A.M. We started at 9 A.M. the day before. So if I sounded unusually depressed, you probably can empathize.

It's experiences like that, staying up all night, that really bring groups together. It's easy to identify with people when you share horrible experiences with them, when you work together until you're all insane. Friends that you only have fun with don't last as long. . . . You really get to know people when you see them at four in the morning. They reveal their true natures.

January 29, 1980 —

I have to write my biology paper tonight. It's called "The Evolution of the Phylum *Chordata.*" Doesn't that sound like a best seller?

Dr. Pfeffer says I can turn in the paper tomorrow and get an A or I can turn it in next week and get an A-minus. I must be insane because I plan to turn it in tomorrow. What difference would that minus make to me?

I guess that I constantly have to prove myself to myself. I feel inferior and can only conquer that feeling with an A.

I wonder what I'll do when I leave school and grades behind. I'll probably have to find a loving husband who will tell me I'm great every time I feel lousy.

January 30, 1980 —

I turned in my paper today—it took me about twelve hours to complete. Now I know all about evolution.

My father asked me if I believed in evolution the other day. I replied that of course I did, didn't he? He asked me if that didn't bother me as a Christian, since the theory goes against the Bible's teachings. We argued for awhile. I said I didn't need to believe every word of the Bible to believe its basic messages. God's days are longer than ours, anyway.

"But if humans evolved," my father asked, "at what stage did they first have souls?"

"Who says animals can't have souls? Don't you think you're being arrogant?"

"It may be easy to think a dog or cat has a soul, but what about a cockroach? Where do you draw the line?"

"What makes us think *we* can draw the line? We'll never know, so why bother worrying?"

Silence.

"Right."

Oh, I love to win arguments with my father.

Anyway, regardless of my personal beliefs, I had to write the paper. Naturally, the topic made me think of the Ik and emotional evolution. Physically, it's nearly impossible to evolve backwards, but emotionally, I think we grow in waves, spurting forward and sinking back. The Ik were in a sinking phase. They lost too many of their onion layers.

Speaking of onions, I'm the only self-professed potato I've met. That worries me. I may really be an onion that thinks it's a potato because that sounds better. Or maybe my onion-like layers of morals and "virtue" have fused until I can't peel them off anymore. I know, though, that there are many things I simply could not do no matter what the circumstances.

February 3, 1980 —

I went to bed at 4:30 and woke up at nine. I didn't feel like running, so instead I called Susie and we went to the Art Exhibit that just opened at the University of Hawaii. We wanted to write it up for Art History.

Frankly, I found much of the exhibit quite gaudy and ugly. It featured some huge fiberglass sculptures with light-bulb eyes. Ugh! I liked some of it—a brilliant, huge painting made with shiny dots; an abstract in blue; watercolors; a strange carving. But most of it I found both pretentious and obnoxious. I snickered softly to myself when I heard two cultured ladies pronounce a hideous flower painting "vibrant . . . exciting . . . alive . . ." Then I worried—what was I missing?

I don't know why modern artists try so hard to be weird. It seems that society values departure from tradition so much that the departure itself is a tradition.

I find the same thing in literature. I write a lot of poetry and I used to use rhyme and meter in almost all my poems. But then I found that people wouldn't take my rhymes and sonnets as seriously as blank verse. So now guess what I write?

Let me show you how criticism has changed my style:

Poem #1 (Sonnet)

I looked ahead and tried to chart my way
To pick a path evading rocks and holes
But where I looked the clouds swirled thick and gray,
Concealing clues from lost and searching souls.
I had to move—at first I crept with care
Testing the earth before placing my feet
If it felt soft, I dared not step there
Afraid of any pitfalls I might meet.
Years passed and I had scarcely moved at all
I cursed my dumb dependence on my eyes
Now I stride boldly, fearing not to fall
And though I stumble, strong again I rise.

The future holds what we will never find
Until we leave our fear of it behind.

Poem #2

WINDOW

Through the dark glass wall I see
The meeting brightly lit.
Tiny people talk with
Silent Sincerity
Applaud, agree and fiddle
With punch cups and crumby napkins.

In the dark reflection I watch myself
Watching these earnest meeters.
The smooth glass brings together
Their world and mine
Fusing the two images
Of what it separates.

If public opinion (second poem was received better than first) changes me that much, I suppose I can see what makes artists hang Crayolas and abalone shells from a latex bar.

I think art is one of the things that makes us human, that lifts us above the primates. No other animal devotes so much time and attention to individual (and frankly impractical) self-expression.

Art is like love and generosity—a luxury when survival from day to day is certain and secure. And like these virtues, it lifts our reason for existence beyond mere existence itself.

February 5, 1980 —
I woke up at 4:30 today and went for a short run. It struck me, as I dressed, that I had gone to bed at

this same time two days ago. I'm getting a little confused as to what is night and what is day. But whether I get up early or go to bed late, I love to be awake when the world is sleeping. And I hate to be asleep when the world is awake—I don't like to miss anything.

This morning, as I ran down the street, a dog began to bark. Immediately another dog began, and another, and another. . . . One dog would yelp something like, "Strange girl passed me. Is she near you?" Next dog, "Yes! Yes!" Another dog, "Here she comes now!" I felt very self-conscious, like people were talking behind my back.

February 10, 1980 —

Today I read *Lust for Life* by Irving Stone. I started it when I caught the bus this morning and read fitfully throughout the day. I almost envy Van Gogh his crude, vibrant passion . . . almost.

Sadly I'm not enough of an artist to accept that kind of suffering. Stone shows magnificently how Van Gogh's sordid, hellish existence shaped him. While the style was a bit too best-sellerish for my taste, I really enjoyed the story. As I read I thought about my own goals.

In my younger days I thought I would be a great novelist or poet. My books would explore brilliant new truths, reveal the hidden mysteries of the human soul with insight and clarity. My first novel would be the Book of the Month. With the royalties I would move to the Scottish countryside and spend the rest of my life tramping through the fresh green grass, traveling to London and Paris and, of course, writing more of the witty, enlightening and faintly satiric prose the public craved. In short, I would succeed.

How our goals change. Were I a Van Gogh, I

probably would write all day, pouring myself into highly personal, expressive poetry. Were I the dream-writer of my early childhood, the words would bring in acclaim from around the world and, of course, money. I know now that I am neither. While I occasionally have poetry-writing binges, I now want to become a journalist.

Time, no doubt, shall find me writing obituaries. Perhaps I may rise to the level of columnist, perhaps I shall sink to the depths of advertising. I will never be a true artist—I [would] need to suffer and frankly I do not have a talent for suffering.

Patty's reference to "work" that follows is to her part-time job at The Honolulu Advertiser.

February 10, 1980 (continued)
I made bread today, when I got home from work. I was angry because I hadn't been able to get into the office I work in, and hadn't been able to earn any money as a result.

I slammed myself into the making of the bread. I made a big Challah and two loaves of old world rye. I finished my book while the loaves rose and baked. And then I am ashamed to say that I pigged out. I am supposed to be on a diet. But warm fresh bread speaks not only to the stomach but to the soul. I filled my soul with the wholesome food and felt much better.

After I ate I thought, inevitably, of the Ik. Would my bread have meant more to them than to me? They needed it more, obviously, but would they have appreciated what made it special? I think they would have accepted a loaf of squishy white bread as readily.

Suddenly it dawned on me that my bread would have meant life to the Ik, even if only for a few more days. To me it was merely a pleasant and vaguely sinful diversion. I felt small and mean and, like Van Gogh, angry at the unfairness of the world.

February 14, 1980 —

Valentine's Day. It normally would have been a depressing holiday for me, since I'm not in love with anybody just now. But we had an *Oahuan* Valentine Exchange for the whole *Oahuan* staff and everybody brought cookies, cupcakes, etc., and we had a big party à la fifth grade.

It struck me, as I made and wrote my Valentines and read the cards I received, how much we all love each other. But we don't show it unless we have an excuse like Valentine's Day.

I went to the Art Academy today, for Art History. Procrastinator that I am, I went after work, from 7 to 9 P.M. I had an eerie, peaceful feeling in the darkness. Then I stumbled on a fleet of fellow procrastinators and wandered about with them.

I've always loved the Art Academy and I've visited it a lot, so I acted as guide. You can really tell how a culture feels about itself by the art it creates. The Greeks have their calm, beautiful statues. The Japanese and Chinese—airy depictions of nature. Early American portraits scowl forbiddingly, Italian people smile peacefully or sensuously—depending on the subject matter. And our abstractions (by "our" I mean 20th Century Western society) show how free, rebellious and confused we often are.

Art, like virtue, is a luxury for the surviving culture. Yet it also fills a very basic need for self-expression. Art is part of what makes us human. The Ik did not have greatly developed art. . . . I suppose that's significant.

February 15, 1980 —

In seminar today we discussed behavior and why we act the way we do. The consensus seemed to be that some nebulous "society" teaches us our values and that we learn right and wrong from our parents. That sounds reasonable, but I can't completely agree. I think we have our own society, a jumble of everything we read, hear or see and how we feel when we read, hear or see it. Otherwise, how can we account for so many values in the same society?

As a child (not that I'm so old now), books became my society. I got a lot of my values from imaginary peers and imaginary "societies." I can see the same phenomenon in the kids I occasionally baby-sit, only with them, the TV provides the peer group or society.

In cultures without books or televisions or radios, the children have a more limited environment as far as ideas go. Nothing separated the "society" of one five-year-old Ik from the "society" of another five-year-old. Both knew the same people, the same stories, the same world. Does our more diversified culture, with so many different environments, lead to a more diversified population? I don't know. . . .

"Survival," her next subject, was a senior seminar exercise in perspective building.

February 16, 1980 —

I just got home from the Survival game—I met my parents and sister going out as I came in. I'm very, very tired but I can't sleep, so I might as well tell you about the game.

The first day, I spent $5\frac{1}{2}$ hours blindfolded, crawling on the floor in search of poker chips—$5\frac{1}{2}$ hours of sheer despair and frustration, bruised knees, jangled nerves . . . in short, Hell. I was the last sighted person in our group (we had to have 50 points in chips to undo a group member's blindfold).

For a while I thought I would never see again. The game became so real to me. . . . I really began to understand what being blind means, at least a little more than I had before.

I wonder if this game-playing is unique to humans. It certainly seems illogical for us to expose ourselves voluntarily to such agony. I even enjoyed it in a masochistic kind of way. Maybe the simulation of "survival" releases primeval, instinctive emotions. . . . I guess it's an outlet for fears and tensions we don't express in civilized society. A society like the Ik obviously doesn't need survival games—their life is only survival.

The second day the game got better. The groups competed in areas like efficiency, technology, communication, etc. For communication, one member had to teach the words and melody to a song without singing or humming or speaking. What frustration! Again I understood the deaf-and-dumb a little better.

Also, the situation made me think about communities without the telephones and radios and TVs and even postal service we have. I can talk to someone instantly—I just have to dial. I can hear another human voice, at least, by flipping a switch. I can communicate so easily. . . . I realize now that I'm spoiled. The ability to communicate is such a gift.

The part I liked best involved word games like crossword puzzles. I dashed through with so much concentration that when I stopped, I felt dizzy. I felt good about helping my group. . . . I'm rotten at scrambling for chips, but I can handle crosswords. I guess that says a lot about my ability to survive. In an Ikish society, I would have been one of the first to go. In our society, I'm doing fine. . . . I picked a good time to be born.

Patty wrote the following on the island of Oahu's remote North Shore where she had spent the night after her friend Monique's birthday party.

February 18, 1980 —
I sit on the beach and watch the sea, incredibly beautiful and blue, too big for me ever to comprehend. I sink into the warm white sand, worn fine by those unceasing waves.

The ocean makes me feel so small. Sometimes I look at the water and cry to myself. I don't know if fear makes me cry, or awe, or happiness. But sometimes going to the beach can be a deeply religious experience. When I stand on the shore I understand where ancient people got their gods. And I think of Genesis— "And the spirit of God moved over the face of the water."

How can we think we're so important when the sea crashes around us? Nobody could ever understand it all.

2

Infidelity

I love the earth too much, and when I think
That someday past her soft brown breast I'll sink
And never touch again her sunlit skin
I shudder. I seek loves I need not leave
And still I grieve. Sweet world of earth and sky.
You promised me so much. How could you lie?

February 19, 1980 —

I went to the doctor this morning, after much delay.
For over a year I've noticed this ugly greenish bump on
my forearm. It got bigger. But I hate going to the
doctor, and always have. I hoped the lump would go
away. . . .

Well, the lump is a tumorous blood vessel, yuck,
and I have to have it excised. However, it's most likely
benign.

Teen-agers are supposed to think they'll live forever, but I'm always aware of death. I don't sit around
petrified, afraid to leave the house, but I still fear
dying. . . .

My visions of death are highly romanticized. Whenever I go to the doctor, or walk the dog at night, I tell

my sister that I'm sorry for all the terrible names I called her, and to give my crossword book to Susie and my money to charity. Etc. I can recognize death's inevitability, but not its reality. . . .

As I sat in the waiting room I thought, Oh God, I bet it's cancer, I bet I have to have chemotherapy and a radical operation. What if I only have a year to live? Should I tell my friends? Maybe I should quit school and travel around before I die. . . . I wish I had been a better person, I wish I hadn't been so mean to my parents, I wonder if I can write a touching autobiography. . . . I wonder what I would be thinking if I were really going to die.

In another culture this minor bump wouldn't mean anything. It would hurt from time to time, of course, but I'd never go to the doctor. . . . Can you see an Ik worrying about a tumor? My stomach is more than full, my house is open to me, my parents clothe me and send me to school. What else do I really have to worry about? I should be happy; were I an Ik or a Pygmy or something, I would die before the tumor could kill me.

Frankly, I'm frightened, I admit it.

February 24, 1980 —
My sister and I just got home from working on *Oahuan*—the last deadline. It is 7:00 on Sunday morning. The things we do for the stupid yearbook. I've been writing steadily for almost 20 hours. My legs feel like lead and my mind like well-kneaded bread dough. Running the marathon made my body so stiff and sore—I wonder why these all-night mental marathons don't stiffen my mind? Instead they make it fizzle and expand.

I think we need yearbooks and term papers and

exams to keep our minds too preoccupied to notice what's happening outside school. I don't have time to worry too much about being drafted or getting bombed. I'm too concerned with finishing my copy, writing my essay for a contest I have to enter and understanding the structure of DNA (in biology).

Yesterday (I think) several Oahuan people were sitting around discussing such topics as the draft, conscientious objectors and the existence of God. We had so much work to do—we didn't have time to get philosophical. It seemed so ridiculous for us to talk about situations we couldn't change and ignore the work we could do. "Come on, shut up, let's get serious!" I snapped at them. "What does it matter what we think, anyway? Don't you think you're being a little pompous?"

"But it is important!" they protested, trying to draw me into the conversation. I refused and made them promise not to mention either God or the draft till dinner time.

In a way they were right, I suppose. The yearbook is not of earth-shaking significance when you compare it to a possible world war. And as long as I've mentioned the draft conversation, I may as well tell you what I said.

I think I'd feel guilty no matter what I did. If I went to war I'd feel guilty about killing and if I stayed back I'd feel guilty about letting down my country. The ageless conflict. . . . How many millions of potential soldiers have felt this way?

Sometimes I envy the Iranians. They get the same message from church and state, at least. They don't get torn apart. But we have two sets of values. God tells us we shalt not kill and the government tells us "dulce et decorum est pro patria mori."

My ultimate loyalty belongs to God. But my immediate loyalty belongs to the country. Will humankind
always sell out to the immediate? I'm afraid so. . . .

God, I'm tired. I'm going to bed.

February 25, 1980 —

Today, when I went to work after school, the
secretary I help wasn't there. My father wasn't there
either because he's on the Mainland. I sat down at the
main desk and started selling T-shirts and filing
papers. I felt very responsible and independent and
old. I worked for 1-1/2 hours and left to take the bus
home. As I put away the papers I realized that what
seems a game to me now is probably a lot like what I'll
be doing for the next ten years.

I want to be a journalist and I'm working my way
from the bottom up. You wouldn't believe the millions
of minuscule jobs a newspaper involves, from shred-
ding secret documents (my favorite) to Xeroxing new
ones. Ah, for the simple life of a Pygmy maiden! I could
just rootle around in the green forests for mushrooms
all day long.

Of course that would bore me—I could no more be
a Pygmy than I could be a nuclear physicist. Once you
learn to use your mind, it troubles you forever and
never lets you rest. I would go insane in a culture with
no pens and paper and no one to read what the papers
say. I complain about all the writing I have to do, but
what do I do in my spare time? I enter essay contests
and write poems and do crosswords.

I wonder if I was born loving words or if someone
taught me to be this way. Logically, I know I must have
learned to enjoy reading and writing. But somehow it
seems that the urge is in my blood. . . .

We're studying genetics and DNA and RNA etc.,

etc., in biology just now. I can't say I pay too much attention in class, but the complexity of the gene has really made an impression on me. To me it seems quite possible that we inherit emotional potential and character traits as well as hair color and all that physical stuff. Actually, the most important knowledge I've gotten out of the course is that I'll never know anything scientific for sure—no one will. We can only hypothesize and back up our hypotheses, creating new paradigms. . . .

Everyone else in my class wants to go to medical school. I feel a little out of place sometimes, especially when my friends look forward to dissecting the fetal pig (the prospect disgusts me). I get As, or used to, but I'm really just taking the course out of aimless curiosity. Or can curiosity ever be aimless? How can I understand humans until I understand how they tick? The answer of course is that I can never hope to understand them.

Patty wrote the following thoughts after mailing her entry to the Castle & Cooke Economics Essay Contest. She saw her entry as a response to a command—mine—but conceded she thrived on "the agony of competition, the jolts of adrenalin."

February 28, 1980 —

What makes humans compete? And more specifically, what makes me compete? Nobody ever told me I should try to write *the best* paper, or further back, that I should make *the best* painting or puppet or pot. In fact, my parents always said, "Just do your best; don't worry about anyone else."

Is competition instinctive, I wonder? Or hereditary? Some people don't care much about anything while others have an obsessive need to be No. 1.

Someone must have taught me to compete at a very early age. I remember trying to outdo my older sister in Easter egg hunts and paper doll contests. Oh, I've had lapses though . . . ninth grade in particular. Then I *really* didn't care about school. I almost tried to do badly. Perhaps that was my way of revolting against my past values.

February 29, 1980 —

Lately I've had such terrible feelings of guilt, no matter what I do. If I put off my homework, I feel

don't look at me that way!
I'm trying!

guilty, yet if I don't have time for my friends or my job I feel guilty, too. If I leave work with some job undone, I feel awful. When I eat, I feel fat and ugly. When I don't eat, I worry about my health.

Anyway, I think my Puritan ancestry has given me quite a few problems. I can never decide what to do and constantly ask advice. I need approval. Actually I think I need a little time to reevaluate my priorities. I have to go to the hospital in a couple of weeks. I won't be able to do any work then so I can lie in bed and think and not feel guilty at all.

Religion, and all our other ethics and morals and standards, may tell us what we should do, but they don't make it easy. When God tells you to do one thing and society tells you the opposite, you will feel a lot of pain no matter what you choose. You can say "so be it" about the past, but how does that help you decide what to do in the future?

In one of my college [application] essays I discussed

the purpose of my existence and my philosophy of life.
I explained that my belief in God, and my faith in a
divine plan, allowed me to accept all that happened to
me. I concluded that I could achieve my ultimate goals
only by accepting the will of God and making it my
own. When I wrote the essay I felt strong and peaceful.
Now it seems my old answers were too easy.

No doubt my uncertainty will vanish in a while. It
looms up whenever I have time to think, though; I
can't escape it. Sometimes I wish I'd never discovered
how much I'll never know. With much wisdom comes
much sorrow . . . or whatever Solomon said.

*On February 29 Patty and about a dozen friends
went to see the movie "All That Jazz," which she
found "quite often disgusting but very deep."*

March 1, 1980 —
On the way home we did all the typical high school
pranks, waving at tourists, throwing ice at our friend's
car and having Chinese fire drills in Waikiki. We never
did any of these things until we were seniors. At least
I never did. Now it seems we have to fuss off all we can
before we have to get serious and act mature.

What is maturity anyway? Can we turn it on and
off like electricity? I think that even when we are
making fools out of ourselves, we're more mature than
a lot of adults I know. At least we care about each
other and, for the most part, understand how unimportant we really are. I hope we do, at least.

I define maturity as realizing that the world doesn't
revolve around the self, as understanding the mutual
dependency of all humans. And to me maturity means
accepting God, but I don't think that's a fair definition
for others.

March 6, 1980 —

Today, while I waited for Dolly, I played a word game called Ad Lib, which involves spelling words out of wooden cubes. At first I wrote normally, connecting "drivel" and "vapor" and "lust." But I couldn't resist making words of my own. "Squeagle" and "quistelent" and "tharn." "Scriver" and "vapicious" linked nicely.

"Ooh, 'scriver,' what does that mean? It's not a word, is it?"

"Sure it is. You know, like 'scrive'—'We must all scrive to reach our full potential.'"

"Not . . . really? I can't believe that's a word. Isn't it 'strive'?"

Some people are so gullible. But still, why can't my inventions be words? Words are symbols, tools of communication and to a three-year-old, scrive and strive mean exactly the same.

Of course, I understand that to have any value, words need standard, accepted definitions. If we each spoke a separate language, language wouldn't really exist. Dictionaries give us a common reference, though, and even if "tharn" is really no different from "thing," the dictionary sanctions one and makes it a "word." I hate not knowing the definition of a word. Somehow I get satisfaction from the knowledge that "ted" means to spread grass on the ground for drying; that a yurt is a circular domed tent. I know I'll never use them and if I did, who would believe me? But to me words mean power. Maybe I'll never use the word "yurt," but at least no one will baffle me with it.

As I listened to an Art History tape on Dadaism, I couldn't help laughing at the poetry. "Faosah grugling thisa thisa!" one poet gurgled urgently. A more conservative writer wailed, "Renegades with purple sleeves, purple sleeves . . . my wife with tongue of ground glass and amber . . . sky with knives it sharpens in my eyes, blackness." I couldn't stop laughing, especially when I saw that the slide of sugar cubes in a bird cage was titled, "Why not sneeze?"

I hope those Dadaists didn't take their work too seriously. Though they rebelled against "Art" and made it appear absurd, I'm not sure if they realized how absurd and pretentious their protests could be. That kind of poetry is so selfish. I mean, writing about renlefs looging may do wonders for the writer's soul, but what's in it for the reader? Writing should communicate ideas as clearly as possible. Maybe nonsense communicates in its own way and I just don't understand.

Anyway, *zwertie quort vapiciously! Loogun lijeen, waz waz* and same to you.

March 9, 1980 —

I went to the beach with Debbie in an attempt to bake out my cold. Before we left I warned her that I had to be home at 3:30. "Sure thing Patty," she replied easily. "It's all cool."

Every time I spend a day with Debbie, I have a very unconventional time. As we drove to Makapuu Beach, she hooted with joy at the bright blue sky, swore at all the other cars and discussed her plans for a tan. Whenever a song with a good beat came on the radio, she let go of the steering wheel and drummed on the dashboard.

At the beach I squirmed in the glare, trying to read *The Agony and the Ecstasy.* The water roared and churned up clouds of foam. Deb absorbed the sun placidly. I envied her ability to relax. I'm too jittery; I have to read or write or do something. When I think, I try to think constructively. I finished a chapter and opened a Calistoga water, swigging the bubbly stuff quickly, like an addict. Finally I forgot about trying to relax and dozed a little.

We left after about three hours. Although we had packed a picnic of mushrooms, beets, tofu, bananas, oranges, celery, cucumber, apples and limes, Deb decided she wanted to eat at the Outrigger Canoe Club. After lunch we swam out to a catamaran and basked some more, enjoying the clear water around us. On our way to the shower, we ran into Deb's parents. "You look like a piece of hamburger!" her mother gasped in horror. She gestured at me. "*She* doesn't look like a piece of hamburger!"

"Nah Mom, it's all cool, it's all right, really." As we walked to the cold water she added, "It's cool now, but tonight I'll be yelling, Mom, ice, ICE!"

On the beach we met one of Deb's friends, a 30-something-year-old man with a teen-age life-style. He hits the beach at noon every day, except for Wednesdays, when he works till 5, has a drink and goes roller skating. When he discovered I get out of school at 3:15 and then go to work, he looked horrified. He invited us both to go roller skating on Wednesday.

I don't think I could stand spending every afternoon on the beach. Like I said, I'm too jittery. I need work. While I don't carry my passions to Michelangelo's extremes, working 20 hours a day, I still like to look back over a day and say, "I did something valuable." I like to feel that I deserve to be tired. . . .

By the way, I didn't get home till 6. But that's O.K., it's all cool.

The Outrigger Canoe Club is a private club on the beach at Waikiki. It's about twelve miles from the relatively remote Makapuu Beach.

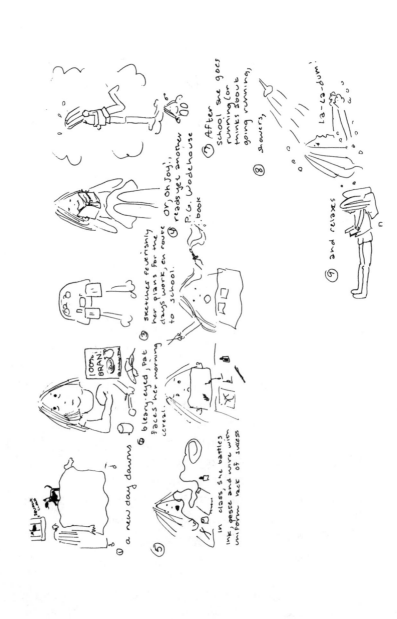

① a new day dawns

② bleary-eyed Pat faces her morning cereal.

③ sketches feverishly her plans for the day's work, en route to school.

④ Or, Oh Joy!, reads yet another P.G. Wodehouse book.

⑤ In class, she battles ink, paste and mire with uniform race of success

⑥ After school she goes running (or thinks about going running)

⑦ showers,

⑧ and relaxes

"La-la-dum!"

Cargo cult, a term that originated early in this century, refers to certain Pacific Islanders' belief that goods would be arriving soon through divine providence, heralding a new era of abundance. The book the class was reading was Cows, Pigs, Wars and Witches *by Marvin Harris.*

March 13, 1980 —

I just finished reading about the cargo cult. How eerie! It made me realize how ridiculous our society really is. Our dependence on material goods is as absurd as the cult's desires. I caught myself laughing at the natives' prayers for transistors and canned food and all that junk and then realized that I might as well laugh at myself. I "need" so many things. . . .

Sometimes I wonder about our needs. Before we invented the radio, who needed one? I can't imagine my ancestors saying, "Gee, wouldn't it be great if I had a little box that played the latest songs and told me the news?" But we say, "I really need a new radio—my old one is so junky."

Cars were a luxury until Ford came along with mass production. Now we really need cars of our own, sometimes three or four per family. We need carpet cleaner and laundry softener, telephones, special shampoos and new speakers for the stereo. Invention is the mother of necessity. . . .

My dad took the "Pepsi Challenge" yesterday at a press conference. They had little booths with unlabeled cups of Coke and Pepsi to sample, the idea being to show that more people like Pepsi. My dad chose Coke.

Anyway, can you imagine how much an ad campaign like that costs? Booth after booth across the nation, requiring bottle after bottle of enemy product? It boggles my mind to think of those millions of dollars (and work-hours) going into a taste test between two

sugary, nutritionally horrifying soft drinks. But everyone takes these silly games so seriously.

We worship cargo as much as the savages do.

*Patty on March 15 saw the movie "Cruisin'"—not
one she wanted to see, she said; it was the
group's choice.*

March 16, 1980 —
. . . [It was] gross. Normally I believe in each person's right to an individual life-style. But this was sick.
People like this need help. Or *real* love. Or something. . . .

As I sat in church this morning, surrounded by
clean white pillars and walls and windows, I felt very
lucky. My home life has been so wonderful. I have the
occasional spat with a sister or parent, but the general
atmosphere is one of accepting love. Maybe disgusting
movies do have a purpose. By showing me that slimy,
scummy environment, the film made me appreciate the
beauty in my own life. . . .

God and religion mean a lot to me. Lately I've
suffered from a little doubt. So many of my friends are
agnostic or atheist. It's funny; they seem so proud of
their atheism. They shake their heads and pity me, or
humor me, or startle me into saying things I don't
mean. "Face it Patty, humans created God." "You've
just got to realize that there's nothing out there." . . .
It makes me sad. I think they're missing something,
but I don't want to try to push my own beliefs on them
either. How can people be happy without God? How
can they think they're so strong and independent and
important?

(Untitled)

Long introspective conversations
With myself.
Questioning my spiritual and
Mental health.
Answering with wisdom I do
Not possess
Attempting to find order in my
Inner mess.

3

In mid-March, Patty had the operation to remove the tumor from her left forearm.

March 21, 1980 —

At last I'm out of that horrible hospital! I can use my arm now, a little bit, too.

Hospitals are so depressing. For one thing, the pajamas make everyone look shapeless and faded. The curtains in my room were gaudy. All the food was plastic-wrapped, sanitized and bland. My roommate watched TV *sans cesse.*

There are only three good things about hospitals. 1). The beds. I love the electric beds that twist themselves up when you push the buttons. 2). The attention. I got notes and visits and phone calls and Deb brought me an avocado sandwich from the Haven for dinner. 3). Getting cured. I have a big scar now, but it's better than a tumor, by far.

As they doped me up for the operation, I thought first of the poor soldiers who had to bite bullets while doctors sawed off their legs. Everything is so easy now—we can escape pain with a whiff of gas. We escape mental pain that way, too. It all reminds me of a poem I wrote a couple of years ago.

Anesthesia

Where do we go when we hurt inside?
We dig dark holes where we can hide.
We grow our skins as tough as steel
And soon we find we cannot feel.
We pop a pill or mix a drink
How can we hurt if we don't think?
Why learn at all if you're happy dumb?
Why feel pain if you can feel
Numb?

I don't like the poem much now but I still agree with the idea. I can't see what makes a stoney a stoney. I hate feeling groggy. I kept refusing the pain killer because I hate that dopey feeling. I like to be in control. In the recovery room I kept trying to sit up. The nurses kept pushing me back down. I felt helpless. That's what I really hate about hospitals. The helplessness.

I really feel for long-term invalids. I can't stand lying around. (Unless, of course, I don't have time to lie around—then I think it's great.) I kept slipping out of bed and padding around the room in my ugly blue pajamas.

I also read two books, *Scribble Scribble* by Nora Ephron and *Manchild in the Promised Land* by Claude Brown. What a contrast. One, the essays by Ephron, showed the frivolity of the media and dealt mainly with the upper class. Brown's biography, on the other hand, showed a realistic picture of Harlem life.

One idea in *Manchild* that I thought intriguing . . . Brown says that when his parents beat him, preached at him or threatened him, they always said, "Why can't you be good, boy?" But they never explained what "good" meant. How could he be good if he didn't know what it meant? He tried to be a good thief, a good liar, a good street-liver, in short. But that wasn't what his parents meant, of course. I don't even think they knew what they meant. Sad.

You know, I don't think we're "good" or "bad" because of what people say to us. I just think we see what works and live that way.

March 25, 1980 —

I think I mentioned Deb earlier. If you want to have a crazy time, do something with Debbie. I spent the last few days with her listening to her music, going to the beach, going out, etc. Now, 40 dollars poorer, I think it's time to stay home.

The point of all this is the conversation we had today. Topic: Theology and the Purpose of Existence.

Deb contended that God only exists for me because I believe in God. She maintained that since she didn't believe in God, God couldn't exist for her.

Now that sounds fine. But, she went on, I really have no right to believe that she should believe in God. I explained that, to me, an atheist is a little like a blind person and God is a little like a sunset or an orchid. I want to say, look, isn't this beautiful? I want to share the beauty, but I can't.

Deb shot that down. "How do you know they'd be happier seeing? How can you force your own values on them?"

After I said I didn't try to force anything on anybody, I came up with a better analogy. I asked her what her purpose was, what she thought when she wrote songs or did papers or struggled for goals.

"The process," she replied. She admitted that once she has something, she no longer values it. She values, instead, the creative outlet and hates to get help with anything. She wants to say, "I made this myself, by myself."

My turn. I *know* I can't do anything by myself. I know I need God. Whenever I play the system's game, I can reassure myself with the thought that behind all the nonsense God remains.

"Life is just passing. Everything just goes by, . . ." she says. And I agree. Life goes by and the world changes. But God remains. God will always be God. I can base my transient existence on that faith.

"God is my third dimension, Debbie," I concluded.

"Yeah, I think I understand now. I guess I live in two dimensions." She laughed.

I can do a whole essay on laughter. But I won't now.

The following was written after Patty typed up a manuscript at The Advertiser *written by a Vietnamese refugee about his seven attempts to escape Communist-controlled Vietnam to Thailand, the last attempt successful.*

March 26, 1980 —

As I typed my way through misfortune after misfortune, I wondered about freedom and its cost. We're so spoiled. . . . For us slavery means a paper due on Monday. Maybe if we suffered a little more we could appreciate what we have a little more. Wang Tho has lost everything he owns. . . . But I envy the Vietnamese family in a way. They know what freedom means and they deserve it.

Parts of her March 28 entry were included in the preface and other parts are included only here.

March 28, 1980 —

This entry may shock you. I have to talk about this, though.

I have cancer. No kidding. I just found out today. I'm really having a hard time believing it, but somehow I think I expected it all along. I don't know how bad it is. I keep telling myself they may have made a mistake. Stage 1 — Denial.

I called Debbie as soon as I found out. We had just gotten back from the symphony. I went with Susie, too, but I hesitated to call her house at 11:30 because I know she needs sleep pretty badly. Her grandfather just died and I don't know how much she can take.

I'm glad I called Deb. She didn't burst into tears but calmed me down. She said to call her anytime, anywhere. I really don't like the idea of telling my friends, but I have to. I would feel terrible if one of my friends had cancer and didn't tell me. I'm going to see my sister Sandy run in a track meet and Moni, one of my best friends, is running, too. May God keep Sandy from finding out before her race. That's tomorrow at 8:30. And nothing is going to keep me from going to the beach later. I refuse to mope about feeling morbid.

Speaking of God, I'm so glad I'm not an atheist. My mother, in a fit of superstition for which I scolded her, flipped open the Bible immediately when she heard the news from the doctor. She found a neat verse though:

"The Lord told Moses not to fear—the enemy was already conquered."

I certainly hope that's appropriate. Anyway I don't know what to do about telling people. I don't want to hide it, but then again I don't want everyone to feel so sorry for me that they don't act natural. I don't want any "let's be nice to Pat in case she dies" business. But it probably can't be avoided.

I'm surprised I'm taking this so well. I have to make sure I stay strong. I have to make sure my family doesn't fall apart. I want to keep calm and not get too dramatic about this. I'm sure God knows what God is doing. I will accept this situation. I will choose it. I will probably cry and scream and I may be a bit bitter for a while. But I will conquer this. I will be strong no matter what I find out on Monday. Strong with the help of God.

I lift up mine eyes unto the hills.
Whence cometh my help?
My help cometh from the Lord
Which made heaven and earth.

He shall not suffer thy foot to be moved.
He that keepeth thee shall not slumber.
Yea, He that keepeth Israel
Shall neither slumber nor sleep.

The Lord is thy keeper.
He is the shade on thy right hand.
The sun shall not smite thee by day
Nor the moon by night.

And the Lord shall keep watch over thy goings out
      and thy comings in
From this time forth and even forevermore.

That may be wrong, but it just came to me and I didn't want to look it up. Good night.

Patty memorized easily and obviously the 121st Psalm had spoken to her even before she knew she had cancer. She did forget two lines, actually, near the end: "The Lord shall preserve thee from all evil; He shall preserve thy soul." Patty, with her poetic soul, liked the King James Version of the Bible, "thees" and "thous" and all.

March 31, 1980 —

They say they can cure me. They don't know exactly what I have or how they can cure it. But they say they can cure me. I have some kind of malignant lymphoma.

I went to the doctor yesterday and he took out bone marrow, bone and blood. He's a great man, this Dr. Mueh. He did a good, comforting job. But when I stood up I began to faint. My lips felt numb and my head seemed full of mist. The nurse sat me down and brought me coffee. I started to cry, quietly. When she noticed, she came and talked to me until I felt better.

I don't know what was the matter. I'd been so cheerful all day, cheering up the few people I told. Maybe I'd acted too cheerful. I think I just realized the scope of the disease right then. . . .

I'm sure glad I'm not going to die. But the cure can be as bad as the disease, I know. I'm scared, *very* scared. . . .

Suddenly "Death and Dying" becomes real. Death isn't too far away. And now the fear of Death will be with me for a long time, which is probably worse.

April 4, 1980 —

Good Friday. I'm fasting and I must say I'm a bit hungry. This is the first year Lent and this fast have really meant a lot to me. I gave up my daily diet soda and all desserts, including (sob!) frozen yogurt, which I adore.

Still, I almost welcome the sacrifice. It makes me

feel less guilty about having so much. And it makes me think more about the dark side of Easter, the passion and the hopelessness the disciples must have felt. It's easy to remember the joy of the Resurrection, the celebrations and colored eggs and candy bunnies.

But Christianity isn't just happiness. . . . I think I tried to say that in seminar a while back. The happiness, or actually joy, comes from the conquering of the pain and suffering. Like yin and yang the two emotions need each other.

So now I'm suffering. Actually I don't feel that bad. I went to the doctor today, for the millionth time, for a liver and spleen scan and a chest x-ray. While there I thought about our discussion of technology. Sometimes our seminar really annoys me. I tried to say, technology may kill, but it also gives life. Lack of technology can kill just as surely. If it wasn't for science, I would have a couple more years to live, if that. The nuclear research that produced the atomic bomb may save my life. Somehow debating seems silly when you're faced with that. At least to me.

Speaking of cures, when I went to church last night everyone (well, not quite everyone) came up to tell me they were praying for me. I was so touched. I guess my mother's friends spread the word. At first I was a little embarrassed, but then I thought about it. It's such a good feeling to know people care about you. Even if they do insist on kissing you in public.

Oh, one more thing, I got into Stanford. I'm happy, but since I don't particularly want to go there I felt guilty and I wish I could give my space to one of my rejected friends. I guess this means I am a Successful Student. How silly.

*Patty's first choice of college was Princeton, where
I had gone, and she was accepted there. For one
thing, she wanted to be near Susie Chun, now her
closest friend, who was to attend Bryn Mawr near
Philadelphia. The decision to go to Stanford was
tipped by the presence of the Stanford University
Medical Center and its respected lymphoma clinic.*

April 6, 1980 —
I love Easter—it's my favorite holiday. I like it more
than Christmas. The message of hope really cheers me.
The only thing that I don't like is the food. I eat so
much, I swill down sweets like a sow. . . . Easter
brunch is such a potlatch. We insist on loading the
table and ourselves, with disgusting amounts. What
instinct prompts this behavior, I wonder? Or where do
we learn to gorge ourselves?

Waste makes me angry. It must be my Scottish
heritage. I can see why someone would spend $180 for
shoes—it's a wild kind of pleasure and a sign of pres-
tige—but I could never do it myself.

My hatred of waste is one reason I'm a vegetarian.
As Mr. Messer neatly explained in his lecture, we
should get our food from sources lower on the food
chain. At least I believe we should. . . . I wish my
family agreed. As it is I eat tofu while they eat pork
chops, so I probably don't save any food for the world.
I just give my father an extra chop. But at least I've
developed a taste for miso soup in my parents and
grandparents. We eat that often and with tofu and eggs
in it, it's a protein-rich dish.

One of these days I plan to write a vegetarian cook-
book. God knows cookbook-writing is a lucrative business.

Eating meat just seems so silly to me. Why feed
eight pounds of grain to a steer to get one pound of fat-

laden meat? Why kill when you don't have to?

I know steak tastes good (actually I don't like it myself) but does it taste that good? I guess it must.

(Untitled)

The wind bit my nose red on the way home
And I drifted in like a romantic waif.
But the cocoa in my mug
Is too warm
And too sweet.

When I stand by the window
My random passions swell too big.
I have to laugh
And let the bubbles out.

4

April 8, 1980 —

They presented my case to the tumor board last week. The silly surgeons didn't take the whole thing out. Also I probably have another right on my rear. Also my spleen may be enlarged. All in all I'm pretty upset, especially since they took more of my bone marrow out today, which hurts. So I have to go see my surgeon tomorrow for a partial biopsy of the new suspect. How am I supposed to concentrate on school with all this going on?

I wish I knew more about this. Actually I wish they knew more about this. The positive side of this crisis is the concern people have shown. After my bone marrow removal, I again felt weak and dizzy. The nurse stayed with me for about 20 minutes, brought me coffee and talked to me to calm me down. I talked to Susie for a long time, too, and to Dr. Morosic. Then my aunt and uncle called. . . .

I don't know what I would do without all these supportive people. We really need each other, we humans. Sometimes people think they can do anything on their own. But independence isn't always a sign of strength. It can be a sign of insecurity, of a need to prove strength.

I think the real strength lies in accepting weakness

and fear and overcoming it, not in denying problems and burying them inside. I'm really trying to overcome this, but I'm so scared. I need everyone. I need all the help I can get.

Dr. Morosic was Patty's band teacher and himself a former cancer patient.

April 10, 1980 —
I had my first conference on my final paper today. As I probably mentioned I want to discuss my disease because I think I can best accept it and come to terms with it by writing. I want to do a good job on this paper—I'm tired of senior slump. I'm not saying that I'm any less lazy than the rest of my classmates, but I get bored after a quarter of fussing around. Idleness hath its charms, but it gives me such a sickly feeling.

Speaking of idleness, I can finally start running again. It's about time! Liz Thomas and I have gotten into the habit (I hope) of running in the mornings. I love starting the day with Liz. She's so honest and cheerful and refreshing.

Too many people snarl in the morning. I feel much more alive and much more healthy when I laugh and smile and love. The mind and the body work so closely. I never really realized that till I swooned in my doctor's office the other day, when they again took my bone marrow. Suddenly I realized how frightened I felt. But my numb lips and weak legs realized before me.

Today, for example, I felt dizzy and listless all afternoon. My head ached and spun. I couldn't figure it out until I burst into tears at the dinner table. Maybe I need to accept my emotions more openly. I internalized them without realizing it, thus compounding the problem. But how can I accept them when I fear them so much? I'm so afraid of breaking down.

The paper she refers to is the epilogue to this book.

~ ~ ~ ~ ~ ~ ~ ~ ~ ~

The Cold War was still a fact of life for young people in 1980, as Patty again makes clear in the following entry.

April 11, 1980 —

All this talk about the draft really worries me, especially since I'm not sure how I feel. I hate the idea of war, but I see the necessity. I'm just not sure it will do anyone any good in the end. *Report from Iron Mountain* [by Leonard C. Lewin] upset me with its slick reasoning. Maybe our culture does depend on war for its existence. Maybe war has benefits. But I always thought we fought for peace, that we fought for the day we could stop fighting. Is war an interruption of peace? Or is peace merely a lull in war?

I barely spoke last seminar because I hate to talk about the whole problem. One of my friends wants me to write a letter for him supporting his conscientious-objector status. I plan to write it—he's really sincere. And that's what scares me. His sincerity makes the draft seem so real. In a heated discussion (my friends have so many heated discussions), he said he would never take a life, not even if he had to watch his family being murdered or be murdered himself. I pointed out that he can say that now, but he doesn't know how he would feel then. Death isn't real till the revolver's at your temple. . . .

Oh, I support the draft. But something else worries me. Another friend, who wants to join the military, was' afraid to give blood. Shocked, I asked him, "So you'll shed your blood for death, but not for life?" He said,

"Hell yes, I hate the needle."

I just don't understand. I don't even want to understand that.

How can you believe in war and death when the sun is shining and the sky is beautiful? Somebody asked me how I could believe in God when terrible things like the Holocaust happened. All I could say was that that horror makes believing even more important.

~ ~ ~ ~ ~ ~ ~ ~ ~ ~

As a senior at Punahou School, Patty had applied for a scholarship from the Honolulu Press Club, submitting articles she had written for the school newspaper, Ka Punahou. *She was co-winner in one category, splitting the $500 cash award for prospective college freshmen. The award was presented at the club's annual Gridiron Show, a roast of local celebrities and spoof of events of the past year.*

April 12, 1980 —

. . . All the other contest winners were college students with spouses or fiancés. My parents came with me. But I had a good time, even when all my father's friends cooed at me about how sweet it was for me to follow in Daddy's footsteps and how marvelous that I had a goal in life.

I saw my doctor there, of all people (his cousin was in the show) and talked to him for a while. The show reminded me of our senior-class Variety Show, with its amateur atmosphere and inside jokes. Just as in the Variety Show, the cast had more fun than the audience. The whole black-tie affair also reminded me of a Prom. People don't really change. They just get to drink wine instead of fruit punch. . . .

Some of my friends can't wait to leave [for college].

They like the busy big-city life. And so do I, sometimes. But even if Hawaii isn't the cultural center of America and even if the job market isn't as big here, I still want to come back after college. Heck, I wouldn't mind working for the *Advertiser* or even for *Honolulu* magazine. I mean, *Time* and *Newsweek* only have so many places. . . .

We're so lucky to choose where we want to live and what we want to do. That just struck me with an unusual force. If I couldn't leave Hawaii, I bet I would pine away and long for the crowds of New York. If I had to follow in my father's footsteps and write for the same paper, I bet I would hate the idea and want to be a dancer or a garbage collector or something. But I know I can do whatever I want to do and that knowledge gives me the freedom to enjoy and choose what a previous society would have forced on me. In a previous society I would probably do the laundry, cook meat loaf and wonder how I could catch a husband. That thought makes me splutter.

Actually, I love to cook (vegetarian food, that is) and my grandmother always says what a fine wife I'll make. But my husband will have to do the laundry!

(Untitled)

How swiftly, with such wondrous speed
Our childhood does flit by
We're scarcely out of diapers 'ere
We land in junior high.
And high school, too, is o'er and done
In the winking of an eye.

And then our parents pack us off
We join the college craze
The years of fun frivolity
Melt like a golden haze
Until we stroke our whiskers
And recall those giddy days.

Oh seize the day, and seize the night
For time flies far too fast
We must not let a day go by
(Until, of course, it's passed.)
So drink ye Pepsi while ye may
Youth's heyday cannot last.

5

Patty's correspondence with Susie Chun, her class-mate and co-worker on the school yearbook, began as an exercise to sharpen writing skills, but plainly it became much more than that. Patty's first letter was written the day after graduation.

June 1, 1980 —
Dear Susie,

I didn't cry last night. I expected to, really. I thought I was the type who cried at graduation. Yet I didn't feel any real joy, either. As I stood smiling and nodding at my family and the people who came up to congratulate me, I envied them their excitement. While I choked up many times during the ceremony, and hugged and kissed people I really love with agonized emotion, at no given moment did the reality of the situation "hit me." Rather it soaked into me slowly.

Walking across a stage, shaking a few hands, collecting a blue folder . . . the action of graduating itself is really nothing extraordinary. I almost tried to ignore its significance for a while.

I suppose we need rituals to clarify our transitions for us. We need a date and a time we can label "Grad-uation," even if we actually said good-bye to school weeks ago or even if we won't bring ourselves to leave for weeks or months or years.

I just talked to Liz on the phone for an hour or so. Why do we have to deal with so much in one day? So many good-byes at the same time, so many people saying what they couldn't say all year, so much love. . . . I stuffed my pile of leis into the refrigerator. There are too many to handle. I will stuff my emotions into the back of my mind until I can handle them, or until they fade. . . .

Tradition in Hawaii calls for parents, relatives and friends to heap flower leis on new graduates.

June 2, 1980 —

Summer really throws me. I don't know how to handle such large blocks of time. I usually react by over-scheduling myself. I end up exhausted, but at least I stay sane. Tomorrow I see the doctor, go work with some copy people, go to my Latin lesson and hit the beach with Deb. I feel a compulsion to pack my days full of activities, to see as many people as I can. I'm not going to die or anything, so I don't know where this urgent feeling comes from. I want to talk to people, but I'm afraid I'll bother them if I call them up. . . .

Officium me vocat—duty calls. I have to go write thank you notes.

To keep her mind busy, Patty began taking Latin lessons from William Messer, one of her humanities teachers, at his home. The lessons, as she will tell, became important psychological therapy.

June 4, 1980 —

For the first time, I have nothing planned, an uncomfortable feeling and one I expect to encounter often this summer. Because I thought I'd be sick, I

doing nothing.

didn't bother to think out any possibilities. That means I have to do the tasks I dread, and try to stay "busy" to avoid, like cleaning my room. . . .

I'm so glad my treatment is postponed, even though in the end it will merely prolong my suffering. I want to pretend, for just another week, that I'm a normal healthy girl with nothing to worry about. It's weird, but as long as I have my hair I can almost fool myself. Only the wig on my desk shouts "Sick! Sick! Sick!" at me whenever I walk by.

People always ask me how I feel now. That doesn't bother me too much; at least it shows their concern. It does annoy me a bit when they say, "You look great! I've never seen you look so good!" It seems as if they expect me to look pale and wraith-like or something, and so react to any signs of health with amazement. . . .

Again Susie, thanks for listening.

Postponements of Patty's treatments usually were due to blood counts not having recovered sufficiently from previous treatments—not a good sign.

June 6, 1980 —

I enjoy picnics like today's; it's easy to spend a day in the sun with interesting people to talk to. Actually, everything is easier with interesting people to talk to.

I wonder why we like to talk so much. Where does our need to communicate come from? Our dog seems perfectly content to lie about in the sun, yipping only occasionally. But look at me; the minute I'm alone I either sit down at the typewriter or start dialing the phone. Or grab a book or newspaper . . .

That reminds me of my promise to myself. I made one short phone call, to you, but the rest of this evening I did not call a soul. It's a bad habit to call people all the time, probably annoys the hell out of them. Now, if they call me, I can feel confident that they really want to talk to me. The only problem is that no one has called me. Sob.

June 7, 1980 —

I really shouldn't be writing a letter now . . . I have just taken my dope, which induces dizziness.

First, thank you for coming with me to the hospital—you did it very well. I know I act calm and a bit blasé on these occasions, but that doesn't mean I don't need support.

I felt rather depressed today. I lay around wondering why my shoulder hurt and wondering if anyone liked me. I have phases where I feel very stupid and unpopular—they usually occur when I spend too much time at home; I don't know why that bothers me but it does. . . .

June 8, 1980 —

I really enjoyed the polo match today. I know I didn't watch it, but I revelled in the atmosphere, the caviar and champagne, the strawberries and sour cream, the horsy aroma. Of course my pain pills kept me pretty stoned.

I can see the warm fuzzy feeling of intoxication has its pleasures, but I can't see why anyone would want to get stoned every day. Maybe they have mental pains as real as my physical ones and simply escape them the same way. . . .

I'm really frightened about this pain. My whole chest and shoulder throb with it. If only I could label it and at least know what's wrong. I can't ignore it. I'm so afraid sometimes that I want to scream and scream, but I can't because I don't want to frighten anyone else. Most of the time I can look upon my cancer calmly and cheerfully and discuss it in a civilized, almost pleasant manner. But sometimes I have to force myself to think of other problems or projects just to keep the panic away.

Maybe I try too hard to be strong and keep too many fears inside. But trying to stay strong, to put on a calm smile, is the only way I know how to survive. It's like a game—get through the day.

I don't mean to sound melodramatic. My world is generally a happy and beautiful place. But so many images haunt me—I see myself with my hot cheek pressed to the floor's cold tiles, retching quietly; I see my hair on my pillow in the morning and again I feel those crippling pains. And I know my nightmares will come true.

Maybe that's why I talk so much—with my chatter I hope to drown out the other voices. . . .

Thank you for listening, Susie.

Ashes

My hands, cold,
Stretched over the dusty grate
Find no comfort in dry dead coals.
I reach for the warmth of flames
That once flared orange
Flickered blue
And I remember their pure heat.
These cinder-grey ghosts crumble
Consumed by a fire that burned
Perhaps too hot.
I will leave these ashes cold with time.
My hands must warm themselves.

6

June 13, 1980 —
Dear Susie,

My hair is coming out in great gobs now. A mass of it shimmers beside the typewriter and strands continually float down from my shoulders. This process horrifies and fascinates me. Sometimes I admire the glinting threads without comprehending that they came from my scalp, and suddenly I shudder. . . .

I just checked in with my doctor. The doctors at Stanford are upset at the delay and think I should have had my treatment Tuesday. Oh dear . . . but what's done is done. I know my doctor can't help but feel sorry for me while to doctors thousands of miles away I'm just a case, a thick folder of data. They don't know or care about John's party. Isn't my mental health as important as my physical cure, though?

I know the doctors want to help me but sometimes I feel as though they're stealing parts of my life. Can't I at least choose which parts they steal? I wish I could save all the minutes in which I do absolutely nothing, the bored hours of waiting in a doctor's office, time spent standing in lines—I wish I could use *them* to be sick in, not the active parts.

Time is such a frustrating commodity. You can't bargain with it. It just passes, snickering as it goes by,

I suppose. Persius says, *Vive memor mortis; fugit hora.*
Live mindful of death; the hour flies.

June 14, 1980 —

I woke this morning feeling incredibly weak and
dizzy. I reeled when I walked—I couldn't put a coherent
thought together. Scary! After several bowls of bean
soup and hunks of bakery bread, I began to feel
stronger. . . .

No one can appreciate health enough. I see now a
beauty in the connection of mind and body that I
hadn't before perceived. *Zorba the Greek* talks about
"turning food into spirit." By supplying the body with
food, air, water, medicine, etc., we free our minds to
create music, art and literature. Dancers and athletes,
with their tough, tight bodies, can express so clearly
the beauty of health.

I know that thought is not new. But it struck me
with a new force. The Latin sentence in one of my
letters, *Vive memor mortis*, stays with me. I will live
mindful of death and thus more mindful of life.

June 1980 (undated) —

I'm writing in the car on the way to the Castle
Hospital cafeteria for a vegetarian dinner with Clifton
and Jenn. Remember our conversation on systems?
Just as I get more satisfaction from writing sonnets
than I do from free verse, I get more satisfaction from
my vegetarianism than from a completely unrestricted
diet. I enjoy finding a meal in a sea of meat—the salad
bars, the macaroni casserole (bleek). Still I will enjoy
walking into a cafeteria knowing I can eat anything.

And since I can't eat anything for the next few days,
I may as well pig out and get even more white and
grub-like.

I actually enjoyed Keith's party. I'm glad you were there. . . . Sometimes I think silliness can be appropriate. . . .

June 19, 1980 —

Perhaps the most annoying part of recovery from chemotherapy is my inability to concentrate, to sit down at a job and finish it. I have spent this morning in odd bursts of activity. I read a chapter and flop down to rest. I walk the dog and return exhausted. I managed to do the dishes—with a break in the middle.

How weak I feel, as I sit waiting for the mailman to come. I don't know why I want to get the mail so much because I'm not expecting anything. Just a break in the day . . . how depressing. I'm glad I don't have to spend my entire life in this listless half-wakefulness.

I hate my languor most because I feel as though I should be able to control it. I want to slap myself in the face, sit up and face the world with new energy. But it doesn't work that way.

I'm sorry I woke you this morning but I had a strange impulse to call you. My whole day has been a chain of impulses. Now I watch the rain falling on the park and want to go run out with the dog and splash in the puddles. But that would be most unwise. With my white blood count this low, I must take precautions so as not to get pneumonia.

If this letter seems strange or unintelligible, call me

It's odd, but the less I feel like eating the more I try to tempt myself to eat, the more I feel I have to eat or perish somehow. So I just made a tiny little omelette and made myself eat it all. I probably don't need food so much as I think. But I do need to feel that I can do something constructive.

A beautiful black cat ran across the parking lot just now, slinking along into the wet grass. I think I will go outside and join it. I refuse to consider the possibility, so far away, of pneumonia. Bah!

June 19, 1980 —

While I know it's odd to write twice in a day, I feel so much better now that I feel like it's morning. It's hard to say anything good about my therapy, but when I thrill this much just to run, jump, eat, laugh and live—I know it's given me something special, something not everyone will understand.

We went to a Princeton chorale concert tonight. Two masses, three other Latin pieces, *Eine Kleine Nachtmusik*, Hallelujah Chorus. All very beautiful . . . Reading the words moved me. *Dona nobis pacem . . .* Give us peace. *Agnus Dei . . .* Lamb of God. You'll like Latin, Susie.

At dinner, beforehand, I knew I was well when I actually *wanted* to eat the king crab. . . .

June 22, 1980 —

Lately I've had a restless feeling, an urge to be outdoors. Last night I woke (actually I hadn't gone to sleep) at 1 A.M. or so and wandered out the front door, startling Sandy. I wonder if anyone saw me in my pajamas.

I can't spend more than an hour or so in the house without wanting to walk the dog or go down to the park and swing on the swings or at least pick flowers. I just went on a long walk with my dad and Sandy. And I have a deep desire to go to the beach. What's wrong with me?

Seriously, I'm curious as to the origin of this new nature love. I wonder if it has anything to do with being sick. Probably. It seems everything now has something to do with being sick. I enjoy the world so much now. I've said that before, but it seems I enjoy it more every day. I feel so happy that I wonder if it can last.

In fact, I'm so happy that I can't bear to sleep. That line in my poem, "Somnolent in haunted hesitation," applies. I don't want to miss anything. . . .

June 23, 1980 —

Your letter about pacifism made me wonder about my own values. . . .

People often ask me why I don't eat meat. It's hard to answer. I thought about the whole idea a long time ago, made my decision, and now I just live with it. My morals have become a habit.

The same thing has happened with my stand on war. The thought of killing disgusts me, but like you, I think I owe it to my country to fight if needed. Now I don't stop to think about it. I've decided and again it's hard to talk about it.

I honestly believe in the creed God/others/self [as priorities]. I don't follow it as I should, but I believe it is right, basically. By turning myself out to others I find peace. That does not mean I neglect myself, of course. But I just don't think I'm that important. To me, ten people are more important than one, even if that one is me.

Life is precious. I of all people should understand that. But Death is what gives it value. If we lived forever, each day wouldn't mean as much. . . .

June 25, 1980 —

My doctor just called to tell me he thinks that the swelling was a bit of gout. He has decided to move me to an adult dosage of Zyloprim. "Still, you're a little small, . . ." he said. Funny, I never considered myself a small person. I'm so much bigger than most of my friends. My doctor is such a good man. I feel very secure with him; I know that he thinks about me as more than a patient.

Sandy and I took the bus home today. The girl has an inferiority complex. "My friends hate me, your friends hate me, you're my only friend, . . ." she moans.

"Oh shut up!" I snap. "Nobody hates you. What do they have to do to prove they like you, kiss you every time you see them?"

I've always envied Sandy for her prettiness, her athletic ability, her metabolism. Now I find she envies me for my hair and my grades and my friends. How silly. Envy never solved anything. I hope she gets over this phase and realizes how lucky she is.

I saw Nick today. "You look good," he said, looking very surprised. I got the feeling he expected to see a wraith. I guess I can't blame him. I probably didn't look too good the last time he saw me. But I like to pretend, while I can, that there's nothing wrong with me. I don't deny the existence of my disease—that would be a mistake, and unhealthy. I just try not to focus on it.

Tomorrow Liz and I climb Waialae Iki. It's quite easy, as you know, so I don't anticipate any problems. I don't like to climb difficult trails without more than two or three people. And I have to make sure I have something planned for every day, or I get depressed as hell. . . .

June 26, 1980 —

We didn't hike very high but took little side trails. The green mountains and the rushing sound of the wind gave me a feeling of peace. Liz and I talked all the way.

When I came home, Liz wanted me to write out a diet plan for her. I did, and also gave her some cottage cheese and leftover pike. It seems her mom only buys bologna and stuff. She was so happy with it, it made me laugh. The small things we do can make such a difference.

I made Sandy feel guilty today. She didn't want to walk the dog with me and I didn't want to go alone. I stomped off, saying, "The smallest things can make other people happy—why are you so selfish?" Later, after I had turned the corner, she ran up to me and hugged me. I'm glad I have such a good sister.

June 27, 1980 —

Today I felt very peppy. I didn't walk, I ran and bounced and skipped. . . .

I love the beach, as long as I can swim and as long as I have interesting people along. Today the outing offered both swimming and conversation, so I enjoyed it. Tomorrow, I'll have to drag Sandy to the bay early in the morning.

I ran a whopping two miles. Well, 'tis a start—it made me feel better anyway. I must admit it was not easy for me. What a comedown after the marathon. I sigh and plan my next run . . . running used to be an obsession for me. I ran at least 30 miles a week. Now, it's an extra—fun and healthy but not completely necessary. And I think that's a healthier attitude, somehow.

Training with Gus

(Written in the summer of 1979 in Scotland, several months before Patty ran her only marathon.)

He stayed late at the pub
No alarm could wake him
But his frowsy face freshened
Once I pounded on his window.
Slapping ourselves in the Scottish summer chill
We laced our shoes and chattered down the path
Eased up hills of rocky green velvet,
Whooping, chased fat cows through fields
Of bluebells and sweet heather. I can smell it now.

And when we flew back through the village
Tradesmen chuckled in their doorways and we
    smiled.

In the steaming shower I sang
Alleluia, Alleluia
Praise the love-lit morning.

7

June 29, 1980 —
Dear Susie,

Today, for about three hours, I felt very depressed. At one point I broke into tears and sobbed for about 15 minutes while my family tried to cheer me up. I can't explain my sorrow, unless it was a reaction to too much joy. I got very inane. "Why are you crying?" Sandy asked me.

"I've wasted my day," I wailed.

"What makes you say that?"

"I only ran 1.5 miles and I didn't go to the beach."

Temporary insanity, obviously. But crying made me feel much better. Once you start weeping, you think of so many good reasons to continue. Once you stop, the reasons seem much less important.

It's getting on towards two (A.M.) and I must get up at five, so this will be quite short—I'll write more tomorrow. I feel left out of the race—I wish I could run it. I feel weird and sedentary watching races. I feel like jumping up and joining the crowd. Of course I feel sick with nervousness in the crowd . . . so maybe I'm better off.

June 30, 1980 —

I can't understand how Chuck, a man who sees Dr. Mueh, too, can have such a healthy attitude. He was supposed to die at Christmas. He was *supposed* to die about six times. He has cancer in his liver, spleen, brain—you name it. Yet with the exception of some dizzy and weak moments, he acts much healthier and more *alive* than the average American male.

I felt ashamed of feeling sorry for myself when I talked to him. I don't know how other people feel around me. . . .

Can you imagine living with the possibility of death that real? Knowing you very well could die any time? The thought sobers me, yet seeing Chuck handle his illness inspires me. I would like to think that I would act with that much class.

Ironically, Chuck McLauchlin, who was part of a support group that included Patty and Don Morosic, the band teacher, was to outlive Patty by more than two years. He died Oct. 22, 1983, at age 39 after an eight-year battle with the disease.

Both Patty and Chuck had memorial runs established in their names by the organization now known as the Friends of the Cancer Research Center of Hawaii. The eleventh annual Patty Smith Memorial Fun Run was held November 17, 1991.

June 30, 1980 (continued)

I had many interesting conversations today with . . . varied characters. I never feel like I'm wasting my time when I talk now, because I figure I won't see so many of these people for so long that I really *should* talk to them. Communication is in a sense the purpose of life for me, whether in writing, speaking or the way I walk and wave my hands around.

I can't think too much about the purpose of existence or I'll confuse myself and get depressed again. If I live to help others live, then why do *they* live? To help *me* live to help *them* live? I'm happier without a clear answer, I think. I'll just continue to set my little goals and play my little games.

July 1, 1980 —

Despite the mud, I enjoyed our little hike. But the fruit trees frustrated me. Mountain apples, guavas, bananas, avocados—all hung tantalizingly out of reach or lay squashed in the squelchy mud. I hate to see fruit rotting—I feel as though nature has wasted its bounty.

I like my days because each part is somehow an adventure—I move from the *Advertiser* world to school to the beach or the mountains. Then I go home and run and/or head off to some outing or lesson or something. I enjoy every environment—each appeals to a different part of my mind.

I ran four miles today, the longest I've run in a while. The exercise helps give me a healthier attitude about myself—I realize that I'm not so frail as I think. When I do six miles I'll be so proud of myself. I won't feel sick at all.

I'm glad we write each other—the ritual of the daily letter not only makes me think about my writing but shows me more clearly what I've thought and done.

July 2, 1980 —

I never thought I could enjoy the summer so much. I work just long enough to keep myself from feeling guilty about fussing around. Also I've realized that terrific things don't just happen to you—happiness doesn't fall out of the sky. You need to get on the phone and arrange the "events."

If you wait for someone else to say "let's do something," you end up bored. It took me a while to understand this rather obvious rule. (Still, I wish more people would call me instead of vice versa.)

I don't want to waste a single day—even if I idle about, I want to idle about around interesting people.

July 3, 1980 —

I just got home from a Latin lesson, at which I did rather poorly. I wasn't feeling too sharp. Fortunately, neither was Mr. Messer, so we slogged through two chapters and chatted over Earl Grey tea. . . .

I felt really gross when I arrived home at seven. I craved fruit and ate not only a bunch of grapes and half an apple but a small cantaloupe in its entirety, down to the green part. I then dined on Brussels sprouts and cauliflower. Whatever was my body trying to say?

It worked—I feel much better now. Maybe we should listen to our cravings more. But what about the times I crave cheesecake and chocolate chip cookies? If I give in, I feel worse. And what if your family refuses to let you gorge yourself on odd fruits and vegetables instead of eating a "decent" meal? I'm lucky that my parents don't much care about my craziness.

I'm upset about the postponement of my treatment and also about my infections. Just when life seems to flow along nicely . . . I should learn to flow with it, actually, instead of trying to channel it where I want it to go. And of course the pain annoys me and makes me grumpy.

I suppose pain has its purposes. I just need to find them.

July 4, 1980 —

My hair is falling out—faster than before. I feel a little sick about it, but it's not as though I'm not prepared.

I discovered the sad news right before we left for Moni's. There the sparklers and fireworks and, of course, the people made me laugh and forget my hair. I thought, these people don't care whether I have hair or not. None of the people who matter cares . . . they will like me bald and if they don't, good riddance.

Liz and Sandy and I had a great dinner of eggs, Brussels sprouts, yogurt, boysenberries, peaches and blueberries. As we sat down at the table Liz said, "I feel like I have two sisters." That made me feel good, and also lucky. I can't imagine a better sister than Sandy.

. . .

My hair is falling out like crazy now, in big hunks. I'm so scared, Susie. I don't believe this is happening to me. I bet it's because the dumb resident came late and the ice melted. . . . I suppose it doesn't matter now.

I wish I could go to sleep and have the bad dream go away in the morning. But in the morning I'll find hair all over my pillow.

I'm so scared.

By one theory, wearing an ice cap during chemo-therapy may at least slow the rate of hair loss.

Small Comfort

I'm cautious now. I don't plan in advance.
Why place my hopes on years I may not see?
Instead I seize each moment, snatch each chance
To laugh. If I laugh death won't bother me.

As much, that is. Of course it's always there.
And when the nausea shakes me, when the pain
Cries out in my sick bones, I know despair
And only faith can bring me back again.

Don't cry or I will too, and I can't cry;
Or I will slip back into that dark hell.
I'm trying to be brave. Don't make me lie.
I feel fine now. Pretend that I am well.

8

July 6, 1980 —
Dear Susie,

I started to write to you last night, but I fell asleep. I love to feel tired at the end of a busy, active day. I hate to awaken limp at the beginning of a dull, droopy day. Today I awoke refreshed and skipped out to the kitchen for a juicy mango breakfast.

Now I'm at the downtown library, taking a break from work. They painted the courtyard chairs a deeper green. I've always loved these wooden chairs. I sit back in one now, watching tiny blossoms fall from the trees and drift to the earth.

I'm wearing my new hat with an orchid lei around it. So I see the world framed in straw—the brim curves slightly around my face. I like my hat—already I feel attached to it, although I don't really need it yet. I feel very summery in it.

Hamilton Library, where Margie works, is the main library at the University of Hawaii.

July 7, 1980 —
I'm sitting in a "Super Quiet Corner" of Hamilton Library now. Outside the window coral shower trees flame against the cloudy sky and mopeds whine by,

disturbing this super quiet. Someone has written on my carrel, "I am in love and oh, how painful it is." From the handwriting, I think I would like this lovelorn person . . .

[This morning] I saw the hair on my pillow and considered crying and closing the door to my room and sulking the rest of the day. Instead I got up, ate a mango and arrived at your doorstep.

When I pictured my hair falling out, I saw myself mourning over large clumps of hair. I expected wails and tantrums over the unfairness of it all. I did not foresee the constant shedding, nor did I think I could absorb it quite this calmly. I'm upset, very upset—you can tell right away, I know. But somehow I'm comforted; it's happening, it's real this time and it was the side effect I dreaded the most.

I felt a bit moody all day and I couldn't imagine myself happily chatting. But this bunch always makes me happy. I need other people so much. I enjoy my solitary moments—walking the dog, taking the bus, sitting under a tree. But I don't want any more than moments.

Liz says she'd like to live up in the mountains, alone, for a couple of years. "Just to see if I could handle it, you know?"

I couldn't handle it. My life-style is so centered around other people that even a week of complete solitude, even a day or two, would shake me. My calendar is filled with names—Susie, Moni, Liz, Sandy, Thomas, Mr. Messer, etc. "Beach, movie, dinner, spend the night, party . . ." I plan feverishly, afraid that if I don't I won't see anyone for weeks, or forever.

July 10, 1980 —

I would be really happy about my week's reprieve, I would be ecstatic about my delay in treatment, IF I didn't have a bald spot on the top of my head, IF my wig wasn't so ugly and IF my hat fit over my wig (it doesn't). It all seems inevitable now; my scalp shows in sickening patches. I can't even cry. I only stare dully in the mirror and snap, frustrated, at whomever is near. This is one of the worst things that has ever happened to me and it isn't even over yet. . . .

Today I heard my doctor tell a man he was going to die. "Surgery or not, I don't think we can cure you," he said. "I just don't know how long you have." I felt guilty to hear this news, so bluntly put, but the doors to my room and their room were open.

The nurses all tell me I am the doctor's pet, the favorite. "In all the time he has been here, you're the only one he has really warmed up to. . . . He's usually so detached," claimed one. It's hard for me to believe that, but I hear it a lot.

This afternoon he asked me how my love life was. "The same," I said evasively, watching him hit me in the stomach. "Do you have a boyfriend?" he inquired. "No." I shook my head as I took several slow, deep breaths for him. "Just as well," he responded. "I've avoided all that myself."

"Just as well," I thought, myself. Can you imagine the situation my hypothetical boyfriend would face? He would have an ugly baldheaded girl on his hands who got revoltingly ill every three weeks and he'd feel too guilty to get rid of her. How sad.

And so to bed.

*Patty's early chemotherapy was rough for her—so
much so that in the case she refers to here she had
been admitted to the hospital for treatment.*

July 20, 1980 —

Sorry for the recent lack of letters but I'm sure you
understand why I wasn't in the mood to scribble away.
I'm certainly glad to be home. The hospital isn't that
bad for one or two nights, but four . . . ugh . . .

I finally washed my hair and I feel much better
now. I am still not bald. I had an ice cap again, as you
know. I keep on hoping. It seems so sad not to hope
. . . here I always think, "Because I do not hope to turn
again . . ."

Sometimes I think Ash Wednesday is a sad poem.
But there's one part . . . something like, "Consequently
I rejoice, having to construct something upon which to
rejoice," that always cheers me. Because I now begin
to know how it is to construct your joys. . . .

Once again, I'm having trouble concentrating . . . I
can't seem to do anything for more than a few minutes. Already I've sat down at the typewriter about four
times. So I'll finish in one last burst and continue in a
happier time.

Time in the hospital seems so unreal once I'm out.
It must be better that way. But I never really understand how much time I spend there, just as I never
understand how much time I spend asleep. Time drags
there, but I don't relate it to our time. . . .

July 21, 1980 —

I feel much, much better now, though a few times
today I had sudden, violent stomach aches. I went on
a lot of walks to get out in the therapeutic fresh air
and I read one-and-a-half fluffly P.G. Wodehouse

books. I also slept a lot, just to pass the time. It's odd how I try to save time when I'm well and how I try to fritter it away when I'm sick.

July 22, 1980 —

My father's birthday passed like many others. I played waitress to let my parents and grandparents talk and also to give my restless hands something to do. I'd rather skip around serving people than sit staring at my plate. I made my dad two birthday cards while I waited at Hamilton Library.

On my way over to the library a strange man stopped me. "That's a really nice hat you've got there!" he said. I wonder if people know how nice little remarks can make other people feel. I thought that was sweet of him . . .

Sandy is now enthusiastic about T.S. Eliot. "Come let us go, . . ." I hear her muttering. "No, it's 'Let us go, then, . . .' " I correct her.

I like to see her following me in so many ways. It's flattering, I guess. I find myself telling her stupid things like, "Always bring food for the staff, . . ." just because I liked to do them. . . .

July 23, 1980 —

I just got back from a lesson at Mr. Messer's. It's odd that I didn't realize how exciting learning is when I learned six hours a day. Now that I rove about learning in bits and picking up scraps in books, I get so enthusiastic—I see the great "Why?" of Punahou, college, poetry—or at least begin to see it.

I don't feel half so sad about leaving Punahou now. Rather I'm grateful it gave me opportunities for lessons like this, for all these valuable encounters and conversations and I'm grateful I took advantage of them. . . .

Sometime before I leave [for college] I will write my "Mango Days." These are my mango days, Susie. I'm not sure exactly how the metaphor will work, but my summer seems bound to that exquisite, sweet, opulent orange fruit. I must think this out sometime as a valuable mental exercise, if not a lasting contribution to literature. (Like Hemingway's fine poems?)

I wish I never had to go to sleep. It's something I want to save for hospitals. Then I long to slip out of pain. . . . Now I want to read and write and dance around in the moonshine. I don't want to go to bed! And I wouldn't if I didn't need to get up in the morning.

I love the mornings, though. Can one be a night and morning person? Why do people always try to separate them?

July 26, 1980 —

My pains are beginning to come back, at least in my shoulders, and they make me testy and crotchety and liable to burst into tears. I enjoyed the movie last night, but it's harder to laugh at "Transsexual Transylvania" when you suddenly notice that your clavicle is tender, when you move your leg and your knee screams. I don't want to make a big deal out of my pain. It isn't the pain itself that bothers me. It's not knowing WHY I hurt. I can't help brooding.

I just spent an hour or so sorting through all my junk and aimlessly tidying my room. My father wants to go to Farrell's [Ice Cream Parlour] but I don't particularly want to. I don't particularly want to do anything. Part of me says time is too valuable to waste and the other part says time goes too slowly.

Anyway I must confess that I also spent about 15 minutes sobbing . . . maybe that's why my parents want to take me out. I think there's something wrong

with me. Lately people have started to annoy me and
that's unusual for me. [In some cases] it makes me
wonder if I'm jealous. I don't know why I would be
unless I envy their carefree silliness. I worry about
everything now and it certainly isn't doing me any
good. I worry about money, my health, my hair, my
weight; seriously, I worry about worrying. . . .

I want to take a vacation from living, somehow. I
just want to sleep for a week and wake up with a new
attitude. Maybe church will help me.

I hate to feel sorry for myself, but sometimes I have
so many excuses to say "Poor Patty."

July 27, 1980 —
The summer is ending. I have two months left, half
my vacation, but I still know it's ending. The talk of
planes and luggage and clothes and courses excites
and depresses me. More than ever I loathe the sickness that complicates my life, even though I understand it has improved my life, too.

You can't separate pain and beauty, life and death.
. . .

I'm completely broke now—I have about a dollar in
bus fare to last me the week. I don't want to touch my
clothes fund or beg my parents for money. I'll see how
far I can go on nothing—it may be amusing. I will enjoy
simple pleasures like trips to the library, sack lunches
and Latin lessons.

And writing letters, of course.

July 28, 1980 —
Of all the positive experiences I've had this summer, these [Latin] lessons have been the best because
they have continuity, direction toward a long-term
goal. Without my job and my lessons I think I would

despair. You cannot live for the occasional outing but you can program your life around projects.

My boss is cute. After I'd cleared a few stacks of papers out of his office in tedious hours of page tearing, he informed me that he was getting agoraphobia from the wide open spaces I'd created. I told him to let me know if he wanted anything else done. "Great!" he cried when I told him I wouldn't leave until late September.

I need such reassurance. . . .

I wonder if people worry about me. I know that the Morosics think I (choke, choke) study too much. As Mark Twain would say, I should smile. And [another friend] thinks I'm too damned intellectual.

But if being intellectual means you prefer poetry to racy novelettes and hate the Village People, and if studying Latin and reading Lewis Thomas make you unbearably stuffy and anti-social (as my friend implies when she sighs at me), then let me become a pompous intellectual. At least I'll be happy.

July 29, 1980 —

My doctor called to check up on me. I told him about my tingling fingers and mouth sore. "I'm not surprised. I stepped up the dose this time," he said. "If you get so you can't eat, let me know and I'll give you something to numb the sore."

I decided not to think too much about that.

As I caroled around the house today, I recalled that you called hymns "propaganda." Not all hymns, Susie. Some can be honest expressions of joy and gratitude.

"Joyful, Joyful, We Adore Thee, God of Mercy, Lord of Love, . . ." I sang. Do you ever get a fluttery feeling in your chest, sudden excitement for no reason? I wonder what it is. Sometimes I think it's God. As my life gets more difficult, my faith grows.

I thought of a tentative definition for a writer. A writer can't be happy without writing, takes pleasure in phrasing a thought well and loves words. Of course that's just a beginning.

I slept for two hours today on the floor of my mother's office. Maybe I am doing too much, wearing myself out. I don't intend to stop. Tomorrow I help Sandy with her newspaper route.

July 31, 1980 —

I finished *The Power and the Glory* [by Graham Greene] and I enjoyed both style and content. It disturbed me. The book deals with a priest in a society that forbids religion, punishing Catholics with imprisonment and priests with death. The unnamed protagonist is a bad priest who has sinned mortally, yet martyrs himself. . . . It is all very confusing. . . .

Sin confuses me so much that sometimes I wish I were Catholic, that I had some concrete rules. My own code is so general, almost too vague to put into words. It must be too vague to put into words because I can't explain it to you.

Anyway, my next book is *Free Fall* [by William Golding], which also deals with sin. Is Mr. Messer trying to tell me something?

At one point in *The Power,* the priest thinks that hate is merely lack of imagination, inability to picture another person's mind. I felt guilty as I agreed with him. Lately I've gotten angry much more frequently, not that I show it. Only when I can mentally become the other person does my anger disappear. If I think long enough, I can love anyone. For me to hate is laziness and if I detest someone it merely means I don't have the strength (or the imagination) for love.

Sometimes I think I can love the whole world, until an irritating remark humbles me. But that's a casual kind of love, not as deep as real friendship. . . .

August 1, 1980 —

I dreaded this day because so much happens in August. So many people leave . . . Sandy goes [back] to school . . . I turn 18 [on August 31].

So I sat at the bus stop thinking of good-bye presents to give people. I sat at many bus stops today and read on many buses and tried to convince myself that really I wasn't wasting my time. I read more of *Free Fall* and ate my sugarless Life Savers and let my mind wander. . . .

Help! The summer is ending!

Lull

The morning sun is warm upon my cheeks
And if I do not turn I will not see
Those clouds, grey giants gathering in the hills
Behind me. Grey clouds heavy with unborn rain.
Though now a cool breeze rustles in my hair
Winds live in the dark hills, winds that can drive
Those clouds to block the light out of the sky.
And if I do not turn . . . But I must face
The clouds, the wind. This sunshine cannot last.

God, give me strength to make your will my own
And Father, rock me gently in your arms
While the storm blows through me.

9

August 3, 1980 —
Dear Susie,

I touched my head today and found my scalp tender. I noticed a purple mark extending from my temple to the top of my head. And I panicked. I called my doctor. He wasn't home. I went down to Kaiser [Medical Center] telling my mother everything I thought the lump might be. Every few minutes my heart lurched and the possibility of death stood cold and solid before me. I nearly cried. I decided to die with strength and dignity.

And I discovered that it probably is just blood beneath the skin. I worry still, but today I laughed in the sun at the sand animal contest and chattered and napped. I don't have enough time to think about dying.

A tumor on the scalp . . . The thought frightened me: the scalp, the skull, then the brain. Finally the voice of logic yelled, "Shut up, Patty!" And another little drama took a station break.

August 4, 1980 —
. . . I returned *Free Fall*, which I finished this morning. In one vivid scene the protagonist, locked in a cupboard by the Gestapo, imagines unspeakable horrors in the blinding dark. He creeps about the

walls, fearing the center of the room. Yet he cannot resist edging slowly across the floor until he finds a slimy object. "A piece of human flesh," he panics, and imagining that the ceiling (covered with more flesh?) is descending, he bursts through the door into the light. And sees a dishrag on the floor.

How many dishrags have I handled this year? And how many more will I face? "Don't Panic" reads the button on my backpack. Trite, but invaluable advice.

August 6, 1980 —

I'm glad I saw Clifton today and I'm glad Dolly came to the beach. They both leave so soon. I know what Dolly means when she says she will go to the beach every day of her last week. She won't, of course, but how can you swim in the gorgeous sunny blue water without planning endless outings?

Today my shoulders hurt; not enough to keep me inactive but enough to bother me. I've felt so much worse, though, that the ache seems a blessing in a way.

In *Lark Rise*, the book [by Flora Thompson] I'm reading now, endurance is the first virtue. "I didn't flinch," the people state with pride, or "I didn't flinch, did I?" they worry. I flinch and I'm not ashamed of it. Maybe I should develop a little more Lark Rise endurance.

August 7, 1980 —

Last night my shoulders gave me the most horrid pains. Unable to sleep, I crept to the living room and thudded to the floor. "God help me!" I called out in my delirium. Then I went upstairs and fetched my mother, who rubbed my back and gave me a heating pad. Still I couldn't go to work in the morning. . . . For lack of anything better, I went to work at 2:30 and taught Boggle to people in the newsroom.

August 11, 1980 —

I woke up this morning at 4:30, downed two extra-strength Tylenol and staggered back to bed. As I squirmed into the least uncomfortable position, I thought about our conversation last night.

I dislike pain pills and I used to refuse them with an almost smug pride. But that was before I knew how crippling pain can be. I agree with your grandfather that pain pills can mask symptoms, but I also want to lead some semblance of an ordinary life. If a pill makes the difference between playing Boggle, having a lesson, doing the show, etc., and staying in bed, I want the pill.

Anyway, this discussion is pointless because my doctor is on Maui so I will have to tough it out on my own. I don't trust doctors who know nothing about me. Forced courage. Those soldiers who bravely bit the bullet would have accepted morphine if any had been around.

Courage is one of the virtues I admire most. It is also the hardest to define. What is courage, what is foolish pride and what is inevitable? "Brave girl," murmur nurses and relatives and family friends. Am I brave only because I'm sick? Does courage come with circumstances? If so, I should welcome pain. I don't.

Enough of this. I got some exciting mail today—six entries [to the Boggle tournament], a twenty-dollar bill and a Stanford questionnaire. Well, most of it was exciting. I read another of Sandy's books, this one about a girl who disguises herself as a soldier during the Revolutionary War. I ate. I slept. I'm glad I decided to play Boggle; it will get me out of the house.

I refuse to let this nonsense control my life.

August 15, 1980 —

When I got off the bus today I smacked my head on the top of the door. My scalp is very tender now, so the blow sent me staggering. I tried not to cry as I hurried home. I called for my mother and my sisters but they didn't answer and I lay on the sofa weeping convulsively. A huge black bruise already had appeared on my forehead.

Then I heard my own voice say, "It's all going to be OK. Don't worry. Don't cry."

When I think ahead, I can see so many situations when I will need myself. Other people may love you, but they can't always come to you. Sometimes they say what they don't mean and hurt you without thinking about it. Sometimes they just can't understand what you feel. I need other people more than I ever have. But I also need to make better friends with myself.

My need has forced me to see how stupidly narrow-minded I have been. [My sister] Suzy may like loud noises (she is blasting the stereo now) but that doesn't make her a bad person. In fact she can be much more understanding than I am. I never realize how much I love my family until pain and despair reduce me to a helpless whimpering child.

August, 1980 —

Hoc unum scio: Quod fortuna fert, id feremus aequo animo. Terence said that and it means, "This one thing I know: What fortune brings, we must bear with calm souls." I love Latin because it gives statements such concise grandeur. Sometimes I giggle at French with its grandiloquent billows of sentiment. Latin, however, has neat, clean dignity.

August 23, 1980 —

Tonight I said, "This may be the last time you drive me home." Then I walked to the house and realized that this letter will be the last I deliver in person. "My God!" I exclaimed to the dog and a large cockroach. "Where shall I begin?"

So now I drink weak, milky Earl Grey tea and muse. I absolutely cannot believe that you leave Monday because all year, all summer, you've been so close. "Call Susie!" I tell myself when I get upset, or get excited over some great plan, or get scared. "What can we all do tomorrow?" I ask. And all those hospital visits, rides home (I'm embarrassed and very grateful for them all), letters, outings and events. "What *will* you do when Susie leaves?" my mother says again.

But before I gush all over the paper, I must remember that you will still be Susie in Pennsylvania and I will remain Patty and all other changes are unimportant. . . .

I'm really scared to leave because I don't know what will happen to me. My last treatment was the worst, not because of the nausea but because suddenly my fate is not so certain. I don't want to sound tragic, but when I remember falling on the floor, or think about my new tumors, I shiver. I can't sleep. How can I go to school [in California] afraid? But how can I stay home out of fear?

I struggle to regain my creed of acceptance. (How boldly I accepted flat feet, a low score, a disappointing day. How timorously I accept pain and the possibility of death—even baldness.) And I sing little songs to myself in the middle of the night. And in the end, I'm fine. But I still get frightened when people leave.

You leave Monday and I'm just saying good-bye to you. But you are one of the best and closest and certainly most interesting friends I've had. This is a very hard good-bye.

So please, forgive my agonizing. And thanks again for everything, but especially for listening.

With much love,
Patty

Panic

I slink and slouch and slide along the walls;
Ooze up the stairs and hide in darkened halls.
I know the secret ways, the hidden doors—
And I can seep within you. Skin has pores.

I flutter in your gut, I flush your face,
And laughing watch you squirm in my embrace.
Who do you think will listen to your cries?
Don't panic. Won't you look into my eyes?

10

August 1980 —
Dear Susie,

Today I cleaned my room, filling two Hefty bags with trash and memorabilia. Old poems that made me cringe with embarrassment, old love letters, old calendars, scraps of carnival material, Christmas cards, junk jewelry, etc. What frightens me is the amount of junk I couldn't throw away. I still have old papers, *Ka Punahous*, even my matchbook collection.

I'm living in two levels now. I try to go about my business with the nervous excitement of a normal girl going off to college, clothes shopping and visiting friends and having picnics. But I am so scared about my head. The purple blotches that cover my head glare at me evilly, defying drugs. My doctor is worried. I am very worried. When all your nightmares start to come true, you can't comfort yourself with the dawn any longer. You have to learn to live in the darkness. I have a lot to learn. . . .

I ordered a wig, long and straight with bangs. This time, it had better look right. My hair is disgustingly thin now, making the tumors all the more alarming. I wish you had been there to help me choose it. My sister [Suzy] helped a lot, though. I've been getting along with her quite well, surprisingly. I did not expect to, as you know.

Sept. 1, 1980 —

I woke up this morning, saw in the mirror that the tumors on my head had lightened and receded considerably and caroled softly to myself as I headed upstairs to take a bath.

Now Sandy is playing a tape I checked out of the library. It features the old radio show "Baby Snooks," starring Fanny Brice. Sandy and I are enjoying personating Snooks's nasal drawl and wild cackle. I wish we still had radio shows. The jokes are just as stupid, but the mental exercise of imagining the setting, the facial expressions and the action makes listening much more fun.

I keep finding Suzy's notes for stories around the house. I read them and feel embarrassed because I know I do the same thing. And also because she models her characters on family members. I wonder if she will write any of these stories.

I have fallen into the trap of asking myself too many questions. "Why do people write stories? Why do people read them? Why do we bother to learn at all?" I supply answers, but they only lead to more whys and then more inadequate answers.

Finally I tell myself that whys don't really matter much. Must every action have deep cosmic significance? We're here, we may as well do what we can before we leave. Stop brooding, I snap sternly to myself, stop dwelling on your own misfortunes.

Suzy, who majored in English at Stanford, indeed did draw on family experiences in writing stories. She did so, too, several years later at UCLA film school in her master's thesis film. The film is about a young girl's devotion to a single book and her

attempts through letters to coax a letter from the
author. The girl's younger sister, by contrast, reads
stacks of books, as did Patty.

September, 1980 —

I now sit in Hamilton Library after finishing the first
chapter of *Journey Down a Rainbow* [by J.B. Priestley
and Jacquetta Hawkes]. I finally found it hiding with
the travel books.

I scold myself now for my laziness in letter-writing.
My letters center so much upon my thoughts that I
forget the description and action that make a letter
more than a journal entry. I must stop brooding and
mumbling and learn to communicate better.

Today after work I went to Punahou and dropped in
on Doc Berry. He gave me a big hug and we sat and
talked about my summer and his summer. I told him
we followed his advice and he smiled. "Writing every
day is important," he said. "I'd like to see English
teachers writing more."

I felt I was talking to an old friend. Afterwards I left
campus quickly because I didn't want to break the
spell. I didn't want to feel like an outsider. "Come back
before you leave," he said. "I have Thursday mornings
free." I think I will come back; what else do I really
have to do?

I walked up to the university, striding briskly to
conceal my aimless state of mind. I passed long lines
of registrants and tried to imagine myself in similar
lines at Stanford. I fished some coins from the pocket
of my jeans to buy a Pepsi Light and sat down to finish
The Daughter of Time [Truth is the Daughter of Time], a
book proving that Richard III did not murder the
princes and was not a hunchbacked monster. Then I
wandered into my mother's office to study Latin. With

a start I realized that I only have 13 days left. The 15th will find me in the hospital . . . 13 days and six chapters; I hope Mr. Messer is not overly busy with school.

This morning I went to city hall and registered to vote. As my father and I strolled across the rich lawns, I sighed at the sunny beauty of downtown. Then my father said, "The mayor has carpeted these parking lots with grass—I wonder if he did the right thing. Hard to say."

We saw the girl at the permit office and she said, "I remember you—you're the one with Boggle!"

I feel so happy now. I think I have gone into remission and I reassure myself by constantly peeking at my whitening scalp. I will get well, I tell myself, for quiet happy days like today.

Paul "Doc" Berry, an English teacher whom along with Mr. Messer she called one of her heroes, had suggested the exercise of daily correspondence.

September, 1980 —

I had my last Latin lesson tonight. May all learning be so exciting and so enjoyable.

At 11:30 the house sleeps. I listen to the pulse of pain in my face and shoulders. If I concentrate on the pain, think into it, it becomes a vague sensation of heat. Someone did that in a book once.

I fussed and fumed like a spoiled child today. I am ashamed, but I will try to put the past away, locked up in some obscure cupboard. Sometimes I think I have two selves; one a child and one a mother. Now the mother soothes the squalling brat. . . .

Sick people are not heroes. They just need a little more courage, which seems to come magically when needed. I agree with Lewis Thomas and Montaigne about death. I am sure that when I die I will in a moment learn to face my fate with dignity and that I will live the last seconds of my life without fear.

I meant to finish this letter a LONG time ago but for the past week I haven't even been able to address an envelope. My arms feel a lot better now, though.

I should follow Lewis Carroll's advice—address the envelope before you write the letter.

September, 1980 —
I sit on the lanai, drinking iced coffee and listening to my new Pretenders album. My face, for some reason, has swollen up and I look like a chipmunk with a large walnut in one cheek.

I have less than two days left, as I enter the hospital on Monday. I don't know how I will get everything done, but I'm not too worried. I have so much to worry about that I just don't bother anymore.

I just learned that I was a semi-finalist in the Pentathlon [a writing contest]. Out of 7,000, I made the top 350. I'm quite surprised. I gave Melinda a copy of my sonnet and, to my embarrassment, she showed it to the Morosics, my doctor and her doctor, who stuck it on his wall.

Speaking of Melinda, we are taking her to Dickens' tonight. In fact I'm in the car, on the way now. As a going-away present I bought her a champagne bottle filled with Godiva chocolates and I felt frivolous. I bought the Messers Crabtree & Evelyn chutney and cookies from the Following Sea. I love presents, especially giving presents for no particular reason.

My father today gave me three records: The Pretenders, Blondie's "Eat to the Beat" and a Peter Gabriel album. Now, if he would let me play them. . . .

I'm quite bald now. The top of my head is shiny

white, yet I still sneak by with a bandanna. We went to the wig store to pick up my wig, which arrived yesterday. The foolish girl, however, had ordered a curly wig. I soliloquized about my plight while the proprietors looked frightened. Then I dropped into a chair and sobbed. Finally they told me they would place a rush order on another wig, straight this time. My parents comforted me with a diet strawberry shave ice. Another problem not to worry about.

I just read *If You Meet the Buddha on the Road, Kill Him* [by Sheldon B. Kopp]. May I share an anecdote?

The Pygmies in the Congo Forest always give thanks for what nature brings. Even in the darkest parts of the Congo, where they cannot find their way, they praise the forest singing:

It is dark now, but since the darkness is, and the darkness is of the forest, then the darkness must be good.

I will try to maintain a Pygmy attitude.

Dusk

The evening slides down to the velvet grass
And dims the glare of bright afternoon brass.
Stars peek from clouds to shine like friendly eyes
That watch me from the slowly darkening skies
And walking home I stop to find a place
To let the moonshine fall on my pale face.

I stumble into the soft cloak of shade
That falls around me as the rose lights fade.
I watch the sunlit starkness disappear.
I like life best when edges are unclear.
And though I love the daytime crisp and gay
I still feel safer wrapped in dusky grey.

11

The day that Patty had thought and written about often—her departure for California and college—arrived with a mixture of sentiments, as she had expected. Most of her friends had already left—classes start later at Stanford than at most other colleges—but sister Sandy was at the airport and a friend, Thomas, had raced there between classes to see her off. Also, mothers of two friends came. Presenting flower leis is part of the ritual of saying good-bye to people at the airport as well as greeting them on arrival.

September, 1980 —
Dear Susie,

I'm sitting on the plane now, waiting for takeoff. I'm not especially excited. I suppose that will come later.
. . .

Mrs. Thomas gave me two leis—one carnation and a triple ginger. I was overwhelmed. Mrs. Kirtley came over with a lei, animal cookies and Gummi Bears. When people go out of their way to be so nice, I always feel humbled. I'm not sure why.

Last week was hellish. Most of the time I lay in bed and moaned or screamed. I'm glad I can leave it behind me. I still have several pains and problems, but I know

I'm going straight to the best care in the country. . . .

We're in the air now. I can see my house. I wonder how soon I will feel homesick.

I got my wig last week and I'm wearing it now. It's very dark. The blonde wigs looked so fake that I decided to become brunette. I'll send you a picture if I get one taken—I look very different. . . .

Between the last letter and the one that follows, Patty had been examined by the doctors at Stanford and told frankly of her poor outlook. Sister Suzy, now a junior at Stanford, had accompanied her to the hospital.

September, 1980 —

It really does seem as though my nightmares have all come true. At least the bad dreams prepared me for the horror. They will try a new treatment on me this weekend, I hope. I have stomach problems so I can only eat liquid foods, preferably clear liquids. Oh, the pain of watching my sister eat frozen yogurt.

After a bone marrow biopsy (ouch!) today, I moved into Branner Hall. I'm staying in the guest room with my sister tonight. I feel lost now because one roommate is playing in a volleyball game and the other is with friends and I have nobody to cling to. Who will eat dinner with me? Small problems, I know.

Tomorrow I take a Latin placement test, then go in for more tests, lab work, etc. Naturally, I can't do everything planned for the freshmen. I had better accustom myself to missing classes, meetings, etc. I will miss enough in my time. Even if I get all "Incompletes," I think I will stay in school.

I know I shouldn't worry. But how can I not worry?

Later—

I just got back from dinner and a speech session [for incoming freshmen]. The speeches actually inspired me. I still want to work toward a career in journalism, but now I don't think so much about the future. I will instead pursue intellectual kicks, the high of reading a poem and actually understanding it, the quiet ecstasy of a paper written well. I don't want to seem morbid, but I must accept the very real possibility of death. And keep my faith.

Whether I die next year, or live to a hundred, I want to create something lasting before I go. I suppose that's part of why people have children. I don't know what exactly I mean by "lasting." I just have this vague (and very human) urge.

Please understand why I need to write to you about this. My sister will cry if I talk too much about my cancer. But she has helped me so much.

Although Patty was assigned initially to Branner Hall, a freshman dorm, she was able to move immediately to Roble Hall, a dorm for all classes. At Roble she could be close to Suzy, to turn to as needed for support.

September, 1980 —

I'm having a tough time, but I will make it. Yesterday I sat in the church for about half an hour. I sat before the lectern, contemplating the words chiseled below. "It is through suffering that God most nearly approached to Man. It is through suffering that Man draws most nearly to God."

Then I saw one of my professors, the head of the classics department. His son is one of my numerous doctors. That man could not have made me more welcome. He gave me a Latin grammar because, he warned me, my instructor is an internationally known Latinist from London and very picky about grammar. "Think of your studies as a diversion," he said. "Do not be afraid to drop something if you cannot do it well. There is no point in doing something if you are not good at it, but give yourself time."

I would really like to be a teacher someday. My teachers have done so much for me. I admire teachers who can befriend their students while retaining their respect.

My panic has subsided into a quiet kind of fear. I now have tumors on my chest and back and the cancer has spread to my bones. I know I will not live to 72, but I never thought that far ahead anyway. I still hope for a complete cure, but I am prepared for worse.

Everybody dies sometime, so it cannot be so terrible. I'm trying to comfort myself by saying that, but I also believe it. What I fear the most is dying before I can tell the people I love how much I love them.

I do not mean to alarm you by speaking of death, but rather to assure you that I am no longer so alarmed myself. I will accept the possibility of death but I'm fighting for my life at the same time.

Today I ate dinner with Lisa and my sister. It was good to see Lisa again. We lounged around her room and talked about how introverted we are compared to these bouncy extra-outstanding types who bound about befriending everyone.

I saw Jeff today. He almost fainted on the bookstore floor when he saw me. "You fixed your hair!" he gasped.

"Yeah, it's different now," I shrugged.

The alarm rings. The sheets always come off my bed in the middle of the night, because they lack elastic.

Clad in pyjamas and slippers, I try to find more suitable attire for classes. Finding socks is the real challenge. Sometimes I can only find purple socks and green shirts... hmm...

Bleary-eyed, I face the coming day.

After yogurt, granola, coffee, and the Daily, I feel better. Thus nourished, I head for class.

I don't have a bike - I try to walk fast.

Sometimes I listen to the lectures with interest. Sometimes I just listen. Sometimes I do neither.

After Lunch....

...I try to study.

to be cont. when I find my felt tip

October, 1980 —

It's a little past midnight now. I just got back from the coffee house and I feel pleasantly full of coffee and conversation. I've taken to studying in the warm, pleasant cafe. When I finish my work, or tire of it, I can always find someone to talk to.

Today I finished the *Odyssey* there and then polished off my poem (assignment—heroic couplets). Then I chatted with a research worker from the artificial intelligence lab here. He had a Yiddish book with him and we talked about languages and literature and pure math . . . oh, I'm happy here. Even if I do absorb too much caffeine.

My last treatment went relatively well. In 24 hours I arose and actually went down to a meal. They give me lower doses now and that helps, but I also try to keep an open mind about the nausea. By thinking of calm places and pleasant memories I can keep the fear from clutching at me. The worst part of the whole business is watching the drugs go in and knowing I'll be sick. But I know they can make me well, too. It's an odd mix of emotions.

One of my roommates, Zanne, went to the hospital and sat in the room with me. Suddenly she started to cry. "It isn't fair!" she sniffled. "I'm sorry I'm such a baby." She wiped her nose. She's such a loving girl that I feel like her sister already. . . .

They have a buddy system here where an upperclassman befriends a freshman in a certain number of activities outside the dorm. Each pair picks its own activities. Tomorrow my buddy, Tia, and I will go to church together. I find church very comforting, especially taking Communion. The church is part of the Quad and sometimes I slip in between classes just to sit and look at the stained glass and listen to the organists practice. I wonder why God seems closer there.

November, 1980 —

Here at the typewriter, I suddenly find myself filled with an unreasonable joy. I hardly feel I have the right to be so happy. Everything in my life seems so beautiful. . . .

I walked by the church the other day when an organist was practicing. At the time I was in a terrible sulk, so I decided to go in and complain to God. The music roared to a tremendous crescendo as I sat down and I realized how ridiculous I was to even think about complaining. The music is so much more important than I am.

I get the same elation from some of the poetry I've been reading and memorizing. The lines roll around in my mind as I walk to class and I recite them in the shower. I want to leave something beautiful behind me. Something bigger than I am.

I know I'm being incoherent, but my feelings are rather vague. I know I will get depressed again, probably fairly soon. I wish I could bottle my effervescence.

Now I am the protégée of my humanities T.A. [teaching assistant] who is urging me to take accelerated Greek next quarter. I just don't know about that. At first I hated my present light load, but idleness is addictive. I like to play cribbage and chat and write extra poems and get eight hours of sleep. We shall soon see whether I am a true student. . . .

November, 1980 —

Tuesday [before Thanksgiving] was our Day of Fasting. That night Tom and I sat out in the hall with what Janis calls our "crud." He typed his humanities paper while I wrote an illustrated letter to Sandy. Then we went to the coffee house, stopped to play with the Wells Fargo automatic teller and returned to our pile of crud in the hall. We drank hot chocolate, read Dylan Thomas, Timothy Steele and Edward Gorey and listened to Sweeney Todd, the Roches and Joni Mitchell.

Most of my close friends [at Stanford] are male. I say male because I'm not supposed to call them boys, which they are, and I won't call them men, because they aren't.

Betsy, my R.A. [resident adviser], is one of my favorite people here. I creep into her room sometimes when I need a place to cry. Stanford was meant for bouncy people. Usually I bounce with the best, but I can't always.

Tom and I love to leave notes on Betsy's door:

"Betsy, I am in love. Is it wrong to love inanimate objects?"

"Betsy, I need guidance. Why am I here? Why am I doing this? Can I borrow your car?"

"Betsy, I keep having strange dreams. Can I sleep in your bed tonight?"

We may not be funny, but we have fun.

Sometimes I get scared, though; I feel that I am too happy entirely. And I have days that shake me. Days I would like to forget. On those days my pleasant life seems so far away and dream-like.

Today my sickness seems a remote nightmare. I try not to worry because I don't want to wreck one second of a day. I laugh a lot. Laugh a lot, Susie. It is more important than you may think.

Patty and sister Suzy spent Thanksgiving weekend with relatives in Southern California. The darkroom is their Uncle David's; David is Margie's brother. The grandparents are my parents; my father, too, had gone to Punahou School, Class of 1923.

Thanksgiving weekend, 1980 —

I have enjoyed this vacation in the sunny south, puttering around the darkroom, chatting with great aunts, getting plump on real food (as opposed to hash), wandering through my grandparents' orange orchard, thumbing through my grandfather's *Oahuan* (it's hilarious and I wish I could show it to you) and sleeping. I don't sleep much at school. It [sleep] is too boring.

Now my grandmother is fixing up my aged koala with new eyes and ears. I look around at my family and feel very peaceful inside. My grandfather's voice rises and falls, a familiar sound, as he tells stories of his travels.

But it will be nice to go home. How odd, I call school home now. It is home, in a way. . . .

November Morning

I sit beneath an autumn tree and stare
Beyond the sky. The leaves adorn my hair.
I pick them out and crush them in my hand
And toss them to the breeze. I understand
Why they must fall. When like the leaves I fade
I too will swirl down into the soft shade.

Leaf

Tonight I skittered home with swirling leaves
And left them in the cold. They dance there now.
I watch them from the window. I can feel
The music of the wind that flutters grey.

That same wind snaps the stars now in the dark
And whips my random passions till they swell
Too big for my small soul. I long to dance
And add my laughter to that gusty song.

I want to blow away.

12

The following was written in a notebook—a journal Patty had decided to start after arriving home for the Christmas holidays.

Dec. 21, 1980 —

Ah. I never realized how much I need to write, even if I only jot down my random ramblings in erasable ball-point. I hope I continue writing in this journal. It may help me to remain sane.

I could not concentrate on the sermon today at church. I had to slap myself mentally every time my thoughts wandered to such secular subjects as clothes, food, fatness and money. . . .

We ate lunch at a Chinese restaurant and my squid would have been delicious if my mouth sores hadn't prevented me from (a) opening my mouth completely, (b) chewing without wincing, (c) swallowing without choking. Oh well. At least the blisters gave me a good excuse to consume two frozen yogurts.

Susie comes home tomorrow and Moni on Monday or Tuesday. It feels so strange to see everyone again. I love both my worlds. Sometimes I think life would be perfect if I was well, but you can't separate pain from beauty. The horror of the dark days makes me love the light even more.

When I start to feel sorry for myself I think of . . .
Chuck and all the people who have to face the same
horror, and Dolly's mother who is just beginning this
fight. God help us all. . . .

Joy. Peace. Love. Hope. Faith. Strength. Charity.
Mercy. Patience. Wisdom. Beauty. Truth. Please, God.

I am not strong enough
Today
To smile by myself.
Come sit with me
And force me to be brave
Or hold me
While I cry.

*The recitation of virtues is essentially the listing of
"fruits of the (Holy) Spirit" contained in St. Paul's
Letter to the Galatians in the Bible, with a few
added.*

December, 1980 —

I cannot stop singing, "Wonderful, counselor, the
mighty God, the everlasting Father, the Prince of
Peace. . . ."

The preceding words are from Handel's Messiah,
*widely performed at Christmas time. Plainly they
held special meaning for Patty this Christmas. The
following poem Patty wrote two years earlier,
before Christmas 1978.*

'Tis the Season

I breathe the air of Christmas
Sweet peppermint and pine
I wrap up gifts with Christmas stealth
And feel the lumps in mine
I carol joyous to the stars
Each crisply lovely night
I kindle Advent candles
And reflect their holy light
I long for Christmas morning
Yet I dread it in a way
For after Christmas has gone by
The winter fades to grey

13

Again, we pick up Patty's letters to Susie Chun.

January 26, 1981 —
Dear Susie,

I have more than enough work now, but I am flourishing despite the pressure.

Medically, everything looks wonderful. My treatments aren't nearly so taxing and the drugs have made definite progress. I have a cold now, but it's nothing major.

Scott still beats me in Boggle but I'm improving.

Early in her time at Stanford, Patty was taken under the wing of a fine young teaching assistant in humanities, Scott Richardson, and his wife Shirley. It was Scott who encouraged Patty to take accelerated Greek. The Richardsons were to become Patty's No. 1 source of support away from home.

January 27 (a P.S. to January 26 letter)

I have ten minutes before I have to leave for class. I spent most of last night working on an English paper and eating Girl Scout cookies. I did Latin and read Dante and suddenly it occurred to me that I like to study. I forget, sometimes, how much fun homework

can be, especially if you start your papers a week
early. . . .

This letter lacks a lot, but I don't want to be late for
class and I do want to get my missive in the mail so
you won't send me any more pointed postcards.

February 16, 1981 —

Yesterday Scott and Shirley and I went to the
Oakland Zoo. A hippopotamus slobbered all over me in
the petting area, but otherwise the day was positively
perfect. The sun shone, the breezes blew and I sat in
the back seat looking out the window and eating
peanut M&M's and Girl Scout cookies. . . .

I've taken to wandering around the lake [Lake
Lagunita, on campus] now that it's filling up. I didn't
realize how much I missed seeing the water. I spent an
hour or so up there on Saturday clad in shorts for the
first time since September. I walked around and looked
at the ducks and wrote a letter.

I hope I always have time to "waste." Actually I
don't believe that I'm wasting time as long as I don't
regret anything I do, as long as I don't make myself
unhappy. I have been extraordinarily happy all year. I
love what I'm studying and I love the people here. I feel
like I have a family. I could spend my whole life studying.

More and more I think of teaching as a career.
Scott has become a role model of sorts for me. . . . I
can think of no better person to emulate.

I can hardly wait for you two to meet in a head-to-
head Boggle match.

Seek . . .

I looked so hard
I looked so long
I looked everywhere and I
couldn't find you.
Why did you forsake me?
I cried out to you
I wanted your peace
I needed your love.

When the mist cleared I
Laughed for joy
Laughed in bewilderment
Cried in its beauty
All around me outside in
Was your peace, Father.
Nothing but your peace.

Never leave me again
Never leave me.

14

March 19, 1981 —
Dear Susie,

I owe you a long letter. I'm sorry I couldn't explain earlier, but I had no idea how to get in touch with you. . . . I've taken quite a turn for the worse. I haven't completely lost hope, but they tell me now that my disease is probably incurable and that I may have months or years, but not much longer. That sentence was hard to write, but I have always believed in telling you, especially you, the truth. . . .

I have had three treatments and two transfusions in the past week and I see the doctors nearly every day. I am in good hands. I stayed at Scott and Shirley's house for a few nights before I had the courage to go back and face the world. My mom flew out for a few days, as much for her own moral support as for mine, although I enjoyed seeing her immensely. Mothers are so comforting in crises.

I have a final (make-up) tomorrow but I don't plan on studying anymore. It's Humanities, my worst class this quarter and my best last quarter. So I don't particularly care about this test. I will do a decent job.

Next quarter I plan to take Latin, Humanities, Greek Religion and Society, Greek and a poetry class (which I'll audit). It's no use chiding me about the lack of balance; I intend to enjoy myself.

I cannot pretend to be brave about this latest shock, the worst I have yet received. But there is an odd, cynical, unreasonable comfort—maybe I should say stoic, not cynical—that comes with horrifying news. "After a time, all losses are the same/One more thing lost is one thing less to lose . . ." runs a poem I read this quarter. Hope, good news, is almost harder to take than complete devastation.

But really, Susie, I'm lucky in so many ways. I have a family and friends that love me. . . .

Love never fails, I remember writing in my Senior Section. How silly Senior Sections seem now. But love never will fail, when everything else does.

I love you, Susie, and I wanted to let you know. Thanks.

Patty wrote the following from Stanford Hospital. Sandy and I had flown to California to be with her for a week. After we returned to Hawaii, Margie went to be with her.

April, 1981 —

I'm feeling a lot better now than when you called. For one thing, my temperature is normal now as opposed to 104°. But I broke my ribs when one of the drugs made me throw up, so I'm all doped up on Methadone.

I won't be an official student this quarter but rather audit a few courses with a "Permit to Attend." I won't be out of this place for at least another week, so it wouldn't be feasible to try to get any credits. Just as well. I tend to worry too much about my grades and now I won't have to.

I had a whole slew of visitors today—two of my roommates, some people from the hall, the lady who coördinates the humanities program (she brought a book of short stories by Stanford writers) and Moon Ki and Naomi from the Hawaii Club, with a big bunch of red roses. Zanne brought me frozen yogurt, which I greatly appreciated as I'm really getting sick of the food here.

So many people have shown such concern, I can't believe it. A teaching assistant asked Shirley all about me and said he would pray for me. My uncle and aunt and cousin Judy are coming up tomorrow night from Santa Barbara; my Uncle David arrives Wednesday; and my mother's sister will spend the next weekend here. Sandy has to leave this Saturday, but my dad will stay until my uncle gets here on Wednesday. So I have company. . . .

After I finish this letter I'll either go to sleep or write thank-you notes to everyone who gave blood for me. Probably the former because it is nearly ten and it is hard to sleep through the night. The nurses seem to wake me almost every hour.

Please write and tell me your news. I'm quite bored and mail is extra-welcome. Thanks for listening to my gushing and griping.

Love,
Patty

P.S. I'll let you know when I find out more about the state of my cancer. For a while the infection was a real threat—the doctors thought it might be the end of me—but now it looks like they have control. Let us hope so.

Patty was later to see Susie back in Honolulu, but this was the last letter she wrote to her.
The state of Patty's illness prevented her from attending any further classes.

Insomnia

These fitful hours I snarl myself in sheets,
Claw at the pillow, tug my tangled quilt
Seeking in bed a warm oblivion
It does not offer now. Where is the sleep
Of Sunday mornings and warm afternoons?
I want the world to wake. My open eyes
Glaze in the darkness. Sleep is a cruel friend
Lurking just far enough away to laugh
And let me hear him.

Deep, dark midnight sky
Moon-bathed and yet electric with the stars
I want to blow like some forgetful wind
Across your face. Oh, let me join the night
And leave these scratchy, twisted sheets behind.

Free

When the doctors finally see
They've made you sicker than before
They finally have to set you free
They cannot help you any more.

You look at them and nod your head
Feeling neither guilt nor blame;
The doctors don't say 'die' or 'dead'.
You can hear them all the same.

And you are scared. They call you brave
Because you will not let them see
You cry. You pray for peace, and know
That now at least, you will be free.

15

After returning home to Honolulu on May 9, 1981, with her mom and all her belongings, Patty resumed writing in a journal. Entries were addressed to Mr. Messer, her former humanities teacher and Latin tutor.

May 23, 1981 —

I am a little girl now. I cry in pain I don't understand and feverish or chilled or nauseous I call "Mommy! Sandy!" in the middle of the night. My dad tells me stories about giant rabbits that want to fly. My uncle recorded the entire *Lord of the Rings* for me. I remember sobbing—and I do not like to cry—"I want to go home." I have to talk about some of the horror. I thought I wanted to forget it but I have to get it out. At home I cry because outside I have to smile and be brave.

"I'm OK." "I'm recuperating." "Oh, I just am through with chemotherapy."

And they press further and in a strange calm I answer. People I trust and know I don't mind telling. But some people can't take it. I'm tired of saying, "No, really, it's OK." But I must.

Because it *is* OK. A profound Christian, I am not afraid to die. But I am afraid of dying.

I don't like pain. It makes me weak and vulnerable—and it *hurts*. And no one else can understand. One of my most vivid memories is retching on a cold tile floor while the house slept. I can feel the coldness of that tile now.

But sickness is not all pain. I found love. When I went back to the hospital for a check-up, the nurses all hugged me, squealing "Patty's back!"

I remember the hilltop wreathed in maile and sun and little gold flowers where Susie and I once sat and talked. I can remember praying in the minster. I can remember green hills and white sheep, I can remember clear, cold water on rocks and sand. And the smell of ginger and roses. And the color of orchids. And hugs. And music bursting out of the organ when the organist took me to the loft.

We always have our past.

Remembering the many positive experiences of her 18 years, Patty thought of the beauties of Hawaii—maile is a fragrant vine—and of England and Scotland where she had gone during the summer of 1979 on her Earthwatch expedition. Her "praying in the minster" was at the York Cathedral in England where on August 14, 1979, she made a donation amounting to a minute's worth of upkeep in the name of her mom, with a handsome certificate as her acknowledgment.

May 24, 1981 —
I am getting bitter again. The Primo Relays were today. Then Sandy and her friends went to the beach. And I lay on my stomach and cried and cried because I am not a normal, healthy girl.

I feel like I am wasting time. Crying was good for my soul but I just lie around. What can I do? I need something to keep me active. And the stomachaches and fevers don't help. I have some medicine which helps a bit now.

I went to lunch at Michel's with Liz's mother the other day. It was beautiful. We sat by the waterfront and I didn't get sick. I had salad with shrimp and a dish of strawberries. . . . So life isn't all bad. I just write about the painful part as a sort of catharsis. There are things I hope I never write about, though. They would hurt too much.

Sandy is the perfect sister. I love it when she follows in my footsteps, being copy editor, taking journalism, etc. And now she will go push me on the swings, I hope. . . .

The swings were too short but I did get a lovely view of the valley. Sometimes I almost wish I was an enduring rock—as Stevens' "April green endures."

Wallace Stevens was the poet who most fascinated Patty, according to Alan Shapiro, one of her Stanford teachers. And it may have been in response to Steven's poem "Sunday Morning" that Patty wrote the following:

(Untitled)

The memory of drugged and pain-filled hours
Adds urgency to every sunlit day
When I, frantic, gather loads of flowers
Only to watch the bright blooms fade away.
The thought of death turns normal days divine
Sweetens every kiss and conversation
I want to make each waking moment mine

And close my eyes with haunted hesitation
Still, sleep alone dissolves away the pain
I dream for days in dizzy whirls of grey
And stumble from my nauseous stupor sane
Yet aching for the hours drugged away.

I mourn for life too beautiful to leave;
Thank God I have so much for which to grieve.

May 25, 1981 —
I have a bit of chill and stomachache now and I'm
in bed. My family is cleaning up—I really wish I could
help them, now. If I could just do something, if I could
bend and straighten and scrub. And the weather is
lousy, too. And I need my glasses. And everyone is
planning picnics while I feel like throwing up.

And yet I really have no right to be resentful. At
Stanford, I said . . . "I will live to get home." . . . I am
home and alive. And I may even take my money and
buy the chair in the Following Sea. *Carpe Diem.*

> *Patty followed that advice to herself—"Carpe Diem"*
> *means to "seize the day"—and bought the chair, a*
> *wood-framed, woven-rope mini-hammock that*
> *swings from an overhead beam. She derived pleas-*
> *ure and relaxation from it in her last few weeks.*

May 26, 1981 —
My mother has a hard time understanding me.
With tears and wailing I finally persuaded her that I do
not want to know what caused my disease.

"Why would I want to know?"

"To forgive it."

"I forgive it absolutely, unseen, unknown."

She looks at me.

And the reason for my illness. "I think it is to teach," I say, feeling little like a teacher.

But why must she question me? I question myself so much. Sometimes it's "Why me?" and sometimes "Why am I worthy?"

I've always been the daughter she can't understand. And I'm not sure why.

Going to school was perfect for me today, though I felt queasy afterwards. I will get strong! I hate this nausea, this fever.

Doc Berry is a very comforting man. He has an acceptance of death few people do. I always enjoy chatting with you and it was nice seeing Mr. Metcalf, Miss Ellis, et al., in the cafeteria. So I love coming back. I guess I'm a true alumna.

I don't get my glasses till Friday. So now I'm reading *The Blood of the Lamb* by De Vries. It's about a girl with leukemia, and oddly I read it long ago.

I am beginning another chill now—hope I can nip it in the bud. My father just got home and I feel inordinately happy. I think I feel closer to my family now.

May 28, 1981 —

I had a pleasant day yesterday. Hanauma Bay was beautiful and I enjoyed visiting you. But I had a miserable morning and a horrid, horrid night.

My mother was tired and couldn't really take care of me and I got up to read and spilled juice on the rug. And my sleeping pill didn't work. So I got very little sleep.

Now I'm at my grandparents'. I think I will lie outside. . . .

As I lay outside I thought to myself of the hospital bed where I lay for five weeks. I am lucky. I used to lie on my back and think of home, of the outside, of water and grass. But home isn't paradise, though far better than a hospital. My stomach had better get better!

That was a very soothing evening at your house . . . so soothing I fell asleep. But your house, or rather you, make me forget I am sick. So forgive me if I take refuge there often.

The water at Hanauma Bay, a fish sanctuary about three miles from our home, shimmers strikingly clear in many shades of blue and blue-green against the coral reef.

May 29, 1981 —

I went to breakfast with my father and we made all these plans to do things that he'd better follow through on. But it was pleasant. He finished my breakfast . . .

But I couldn't go to graduation. I got a fever and my parents said "No!" I felt like being nothing, doing nothing, so my mother rubbed me with alcohol for a while (but never long enough). And I went to bed early (I've given up sleeping pills) and woke up often. But I made it through the night, even though I napped all morning.

Patty, a member of the Class of 1980, had many friends in the Class of 1981. So she was clearly disappointed to miss graduation and the joy of giving leis to people who had honored her as a graduate a year earlier.

June 1, 1981 —

Life isn't fair. My ribs hurt now. My doctor is back and God knows what they will do to me. So I pray and pray. What else do you do? . . .

Life is not fair. . . .

June 6, 1981 —

. . . Especially when you lose your journal for six days and cannot rant about the anemia that weakens you, the terrible transfusion, the pain in your ribs and head and the persistent lack of appetite. I still spend most of the day sleeping. I tire easily, cannot concentrate as well.

Sometimes I feel the struggle isn't worth it. I felt that way today so I called Susie and we drove around trying to find something I could eat. Finally we found a coffee shop where I ate one-third of my meal. Oh well. Susie is a good friend. She took my mind off my despair.

That was the last entry in her last journal. . . .

When Patty died June 20 in the hospital, Margie and I were with her, along with a very kind nurse. It was a half hour before sunrise.

~ ~ ~ ~ ~ ~ ~ ~ ~ ~

Haiku

Salt surge of water
Cool on my tired feet
I have come home.

In Remembrance

Memorial services for Patty were held June 30, 1981, at Punahou School's Thurston Memorial Chapel. About 500 people came. We asked Susie Chun, with whom Patty had shared so much, to share some of her thoughts. She wrote this:

When we were eighth graders, Patty and I planned to write a novel. It was Patty's idea: she was the thinker and planner who coaxed me into writing the first chapter while she wrote the second, third and fourth. We never did get past chapter four, though as tenth graders we made a few futile stabs at completing our book.

It was *like* Patricia to have big plans, though. And actually, more often than not, her plans became successful parties, events and projects. She planned and organized feverishly: picnics, visits to the Art Academy, hikes. She wrote once that, "I've realized that terrific things don't just happen to you—happiness doesn't fall out of the sky. You need to get on the phone and arrange the events." So she did. I remember that Patricia admired Ulysses, in Tennyson's poem: "I will drink life to the lees," he said.

Patty had real plans for last summer, our last summer before we left Hawaii for college on the Mainland. We were to write to each other daily, though we would both be spending the summer at home. Letter writing, Patty assured me, would be "good practice." For Patty, whose life was complicated by her cancer and chemotherapy treatments, the letter writing was "good therapy," too. She wrote to me about the pain and the fear, but because I had no answers for her, I wrote back about politics and sex and the books I was reading. And I signed my letters the same way she did: "Thank you for listening."

I learned a lot about Patty through those letters: I was very lucky to be able to share her gift for finding the best in every situation. On July 27, a day which had been particularly difficult for her, she wrote:

> I loathe the sickness that complicates my life, even though I understand it has improved my life, too. You can't separate pain and beauty, life and death.

Patty learned to take advantage of her "well" days, scheduling those days so full of activities that her friends could hardly keep up with her. She explained:

> It's hard to say anything good about my therapy, but when I thrill this much just to run, jump, eat, laugh and live, I know it's given me something special—something not everyone will understand.

I miss Patty terribly. Dozens of times this week I've thought "Call Patty!" or "Tell Pat!" when I've had something special to share. When I miss her most, I remind myself of something she said in her last letter before I left for college last summer. "I must remember that you will still be Susie in Pennsylvania and I will remain Patty and all other changes are unimportant," she wrote.

For me, even now, Patty is still Patty and I feel she is very close as I read through her letters, smiling at her advice to "Laugh a lot, Susie. It is more important than you may think."

She will be close the next time I complete the Sunday crossword. I will remember the time we sat side by side at the beach, ignoring our friends in the water, collaborating on a particularly difficult puzzle. And I think that she will be close to all of us the next time we spend Sunday at a Mokuleia polo match. We will remember her at a match we went to last year, eating strawberries, drinking champagne, ignoring the match but chatting happily with everyone.

One more thing. Patricia worried that she would die before she did something "important." In September, she wrote:

Whether I die next year, or live to a hundred, I want to create something lasting before I go. I suppose that's part of why people have children. I don't know exactly what I mean by "lasting." I just have this vague (and very human) urge.

By the time we were seniors, Patty no longer wanted to finish the novel. "Maybe a short story," she'd joke, "or maybe a poem." But I don't think Patty was referring to either the novel or the short story when she wrote of "something lasting." I have a feeling I won't articulate this too well. Perhaps it would be best to quote Pat just once more.

In March, she found out that her cancer was probably incurable. She wrote me a long letter, explaining and concluded by saying:

But really, Susie, I'm lucky in so many ways. I have a family and friends that love me. Love never fails, I remember writing in my Senior Section. How silly Senior Sections seem now. But love never will fail, when everything else does.

Pat taught us all that love never fails: I hope, and think, that Patty did know how long her love will last.

~ ~ ~ ~ ~ ~ ~ ~ ~ ~

Several weeks later, the other "Susie" in Patty's life, her older sister Suzy, wrote this remembrance.

I tell my sister "I love you" more now than I did while she was alive. "I love you, Patty." I say it after I've gone to bed when, alone in the dark, I miss her most. Sometimes she answers me, not as a faint and ghostly voice, but as a surge of joy.

I remember the day we found out how serious her cancer was. Patty and I had just gone off to college together and I sat in the waiting room of the university medical center while doctors examined her. I waited a long time. At last the doctor came out and told me what he had just told Patty—that there was a good chance she would die within a year or two. He took me in to see her. She lay on the examination table, crying quietly.

"Patty," I said. "Patty, Patty." I stroked her wispy head, already mostly bald from the chemotherapy she had been getting and I laid my cheek next to hers. We both cried. "I love you, Suzy," she said. I think that was the first time she had ever told me that.

Until then, we weren't very close. We both liked reading and writing, both enjoyed school and had similar opinions about art, politics and religion, but we had disastrously different personalities. I thought she was a goody-goody; she thought I was a big-mouthed brat. We each had a point.

When we were little, our frequent fights had a predictable pattern. She would do something happy and innocent, like hum or tap her fingers on the table. Who knows whether these things were meant to annoy me, but they did. I'd tell her "Stop it." She wouldn't. I'd hit her (moderately hard). She'd crumple to the floor. Mom would spank me and send me to my room and then attend to the wounded Patty. Variations of this pattern continued for years.

In junior high school Patty wisely chose to avoid me. A big sister like this she didn't need. Not until I had finished high school did we spend much time together. At the beach or shopping, we chattered about clothes and analyzed our favorite books, and I tried not to talk too loudly.

But at college we really became friends. At doctors' urging, we lived in the same dorm, and at first we ate all our meals together and she came over to my room every evening. I accompanied her to the med center for her weekly chemotherapy treatments. After a couple of weeks I saw her less because she had met most of the people in her hall and didn't need me around.

Patty made friends easily. Graciously she left her coffeemaker out in the hall and she and her friends would sit around until three in the morning drinking coffee, joking and laughing but also talking frankly about cancer and death. I came around mostly to borrow her electric typewriter. When I returned it we would give each other brief updates on ourselves. "I have insomnia." "The class liked my poem!"

We did have some longer moments together, especially during the Thanksgiving weekend we spent visiting my aunt and uncle. I remember two times in particular.

First, I should mention a couple of things. One, Patty adored my Uncle David. Two, Patty was a weight fanatic. She did not eat meat, nuts, butter, salad dressing, egg yolks or even low-fat milk (only skim). She drank huge quantities of black coffee and diet soda. She totalled each day's calories (1/2-cup cottage cheese — 98; 1 glass O.J. — 85; etc.) every day, holidays included. She was not fat. She had gained no more than a few pounds at college.

A few hours before Thanksgiving dinner, in front of all the guests, Uncle David leans over to Patty, pinches her thigh and says affectionately, "Getting a little cheeky, aren't you?" Patty is speechless. She murmurs "excuse me" and dashes up the stairs and into the guest bathroom. I go running after her. "You're not fat, Patty! You're thin! I swear! Don't listen to him!"

Patty is sobbing. "I know I'm silly," she says. "I can't help it." Then Uncle David comes up and puts his arm around her silently, maybe because he doesn't want to risk saying anything more. Finally Patty starts to laugh, a polite little snicker, and then I laugh, and then we're all laughing hysterically as if this were the happiest moment of our lives.

The next night, as we were getting ready for bed, my sister asked to see the short story I had been agonizing over.

"It's too crummy."

"Please?"

"I don't like to show people my writing. Especially you, because your stuff is so good."

"Suzy," she told me, "the whole point of writing is to share it. If you don't share it, why bother? And how will you know if it's good or bad unless people tell you?"

"This is bad."

"You can never be objective about your own writing. Maybe you just hate it because you've been working on it too long."

"Nope."

"I show people my poems all the time, whether I like them or not." She paused. "How do you like this one?"

> "Above my head the bright blue sky
> Below my feet the grass
> I rest upon a sun-warmed rock . . . "

"Oh Patty, stop showing off," I snapped.

She looked at me. "You're mean," she said and disappeared into the bathroom.

I began to cry. "I *know* I'm mean," I sobbed to the empty room. "Why am I so mean? Why?"

Patty was singing in the shower. She came out wrapped in a towel, dripping, her face pink, her head smooth and bare. "I'm sorry, Suzy," she said. "It's just that it's *hard* to recite poetry. Reciting poetry is like exposing . . . it's like going around *bald*."

"I know," I said. "Don't say you're sorry, because I'm the one who's sorry." I asked her to recite her poem again and she did. She called it "HIKE."

> Above my head the bright blue sky
> Below my feet the grass
> I rest upon a sun-warmed rock
> And feel the wind blow past.
>
> I stretch my palms out to the falls
> And splash my weary feet
> I cup my hands and wet my throat
> With water cool and sweet.

Someday I'll sleep below the grass
And dance above the sky
But now I lie between the two
And let the wind blow by.

"I like the last stanza best," I said.

"Me too."

I was in Paris working as an *au pair* when Patty died. My parents said it was better that way. She had been depressed and in pain for the last couple of months and her disposition might have hurt the budding friendship. And in France I didn't have to see her suffer.

After I got the phone call for which I had been prepared, I drew a warm bath and lay in it for a long time, motionless, thinking absolutely nothing, as though I had died myself. I dressed slowly, then walked to the church next door. The sky was still and pale grey. The church was empty except for an old woman huddled in a shawl. I knelt and said a long prayer.

When I left, the sun was peeking through the clouds. I walked briskly in the opposite direction from which I had come and thought that one good thing about sorrow was that it brought you nearer to God.

We buried Patty next to my great-grandparents in a cemetery in Nuuanu Valley, one of the greenest parts of the island of Oahu. I was there for the service. The wind was brisk that day, blowing billows of white across the bright blue sky. Until then I had shivered at the sight of a cemetery. But here death seemed natural and good.

Following the cemetery service, we had a memorial service at Patty's high school chapel. The guests lined up afterward to give us hugs—my mother and father and Sandy and me. Everyone was laughing with tears in their eyes and I was kissing people I didn't even know. "Didn't that remind you of what going to heaven must be like?" I asked my family. "All that love." They knew what I meant.

I guess we're all thinking more about heaven these days. A few weeks ago, my sister Sandy and I were riding the bus home from the library in the early evening. "Hey, look," said Sandy, pointing to a patch of golden sunlight streaming through the rosy sky. "It kind of looks like heaven, doesn't it?"

I squinted at the sun, smiled, and nodded.

Epilogue

Patty wrote this essay on coping with her cancer for her humanities class in the spring of 1980.

We can only improve when life challenges us. A student grows intellectually in preparing for exams and an athlete develops physically in training for an important game. In the same way, we gain spiritual and emotional strength in the process of accepting and overcoming a crisis.

The discovery that I have malignant lymphoma, a curable type of cancer, began a series of crises both physical and psychological. After a barrage of painful tests, including a spinal tap, a lymphangiogram, sampling of bone marrow and blood and three tissue biopsies, I now face a grueling eight months of chemotherapy and its side effects. The resulting trauma has both tested and strengthened my faith in God, myself and humankind.

I do not want to sound like a little angel. I have cried, cursed, complained and felt sorry for myself. But in a sense the same disease that eats my body has nourished my spirit. In this paper I want to explore the positive aspects of my disease.

I think my generation values independence and self-reliance so much that it sometimes forgets how much we humans need each other. Until my illness, I never fully realized the importance of love, compassion and human contact. I do not know if I could have remained sane during the first shock-filled weeks, or even how sane I would be now, without the support of my family, friends, teachers, doctors and nurses. Even complete strangers have shown a concern that overwhelms me.

One of the most helpful people has been Dr. Morosic (my band teacher), a patient of the same oncologist who treats me. I often talk with him before class or on the phone and he and his wife came to visit me in the hospital. He understands my emotions and by sharing his experiences with me he has relieved much of my uncertainty and loneliness. He told me about each test before I went through it, so I knew what to expect. And after talking to him, I no longer feel like a freak.

Cancer has been so over-dramatized that when some people learn you have it they immediately assume the worst and wait for you to waste away. I feel much better knowing someone who has learned to live with cancer and who has a healthy, positive attitude toward life.

My doctors and nurses have also helped me enormously by treating me as a person and not just a patient. My nurse for the lymphangiogram, Melinda, learned I was in the hospital a few days after the test and rushed up to see me when she got off work. We talked for over an hour about running, food and her home in Canada until I thought of her as a friend. My nurse for the breast biopsy, a charming nanny-type from Cheshire, saw me wilting in the waiting room the day after my spinal tap and quickly found a bed and tucked me into it.

And my oncologist, Dr. Mueh, considers my psychological, as well as physical, health. He makes sure I understand the basics of the disease and its treatment. And he has done everything feasible to make sure I can graduate with my own hair on my head. Technology may make cures possible, but only understanding humans can make all that they involve bearable.

My friends and family have cheered me up with visits, telephone calls, flowers and their willingness to listen. With extensions and extra-credit, my teachers have kept me from flunking out. Strangers, too, have acted like old friends. The owners of a wig store in California sold me a human-hair wig worth well over a hundred dollars for only five when they understood why, and how soon, I needed it.

This support I have received from others has increased my love and respect for all humankind. Ironically, though, I often find myself supporting others in a reversal of the expected roles.

I decided to discuss my situation frankly to prevent sensational rumors from spreading the news instead. People who learn about my sickness from someone else inevitably react with much more horror than people I tell myself. I suppose my solid presence reassures. Still, many people respond with an anguish I cannot bear. They don't know what to say to me. I force myself to stay calm and brave for their sake.

On my first day back at school, one of my friends ran up to ask about my arm. Reluctantly, I told her, and she immediately burst into tears. I tried to soothe her by emphasizing the positive prognosis and the curable nature of lymphomas in general. She slowly brightened and left for class when I promised to call her after my doctor's appointment that afternoon. I watched her as she walked away and realized that for the first time that day, I had completely forgotten my own fear.

I have encountered the same situation countless times since and always with the same paradoxical result. In comforting the people who want to comfort me, I comfort myself.

After my spinal tap at Stanford, I returned to my sister's dorm room and flopped down on the bed for the prescribed six hours of rest. A tactless girl from down the hall wandered in with a huge French dictionary over her arm. "Suzanne, who bit your sister?" she inquired, noting the lymphangiogram incisions on my feet. "And why is she lying there like that?"

While my sister bristled, I replied, "The cuts are from my x-ray test and I'm lying here because I just had a spinal tap."

"Suzanne, you never told me your sister was sick!" the girl said reproachfully. She looked at me with curiosity. "Why aren't you screaming?" she demanded. "I would be such a baby. . . . How do you stand it?"

I thought as I tried to answer her. I think we all have more strength than we realize. We just don't notice it until we need it. Before I knew that I had cancer, I thought it was the worst thing that could ever happen to me. I have it, though, and I haven't collapsed. I imagined losing my hair only in nightmares. But in a few weeks I will have become completely bald and I do not plan to collapse.

A certain joy comes with bearing the unbearable. All my other problems seem to shrink. If I can get through the next two weeks and graduate (with honors?), I can get through the next eight months. And if I get through the next eight months, I can do anything.

Ultimately, my strength comes from my faith in

God. Cancer demands enormous faith, because nobody knows enough to give any sure answers. My doctors know they can cure me for now. They feel confident of their ability to keep me cured for the next two years. But the years after that gape at me, black and uncertain, in my sleep. Only faith can fill that hole.

Of course, I sometimes want to yell up at the sky, "Couldn't you have waited a year or two? Couldn't you have waited till after graduation?" But when I stop and think of how much God has given me and how much worse my situation could be, I have to whisper a thank you instead.

The fear of death has made me appreciate my life. I cannot walk across the campus now without thanking God that I can walk and go to school. I ate a strawberry yesterday and somehow the color and flavor made me bubble over with joy at being alive.

My life may be more painful now, but it also is more beautiful.

Patty (at right, wearing a wig) and Suzy (center) come home from Stanford for Christmas in Honolulu. They are greeted by Sandy, Kit and Margie (l. to r.)

August 2, 1980

Dear Susie,

I found a mango today, dropped by God into the soft arms of a shrub. It glowed red, orange and green and warmed my hand with the sun's heat. As I nibbled at the juicy flesh, I thanked God for everything God gently lets fall in my path.

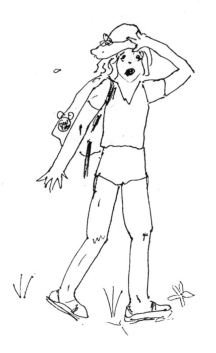

The world is full of flowers for my hat and wonderful people to talk to . . . and perfect mangoes.

Love!